MACHINE LEARNING
IN AFRICAN MARKETS

MONSURU DUROJAIYE OLALEKAN

Copyright © 2024. All rights reserved.

No part of this book may be reproduced or transmitted in any form or by any means, electronic or mechanical, including photocopying, recording, or by any information storage and retrieval system, without permission in writing from the Copyright owner.

Any information is to be used for educational and information purposes only. It should never be substituted for financial advice.

The author or publisher does not in any way endorse any commercial products or services linked from other websites to this book.

Globally Available

ISBN: 978-8-4678-7052-7

Published in Nigeria in 2024

A catalogue record of this book will be available from the National Library of Nigeria

TABLE OF CONTENTS

PREFACE _____ iv

INTRODUCTION _____ vi

1. Introduction To Machine Learning and African Markets _____ 1
2. Opportunities for Machine Learning in Africa _____ 7
3. Challenges Facing Machine Learning in African Markets _____ 14
4. Data Availability and Quality in Africa _____ 21
5. Machine Learning for Financial Inclusion in Africa _____ 28
6. Agriculture and Machine Learning: Feeding the Continent _____ 34
7. Machine Learning in Healthcare: Tackling Africa's Health Challenges _____ 39
8. Education and Skill Development for Machine Learning in Africa   44
9. Smart Cities in Africa: Leveraging Machine Learning for Urbanization _____ 49
10. Machine Learning and Renewable Energy in Africa _____ 55
11. Machine Learning for Environmental Sustainability in Africa ___ 61
12. Policy and Regulation for Machine Learning in African Markets _ 66
13. Case Studies: Successful Machine Learning Applications in Africa _____ 72
14. The Future of Machine Learning in Africa _____ 77
15. Unlocking Africa's Potential with Machine Learning _____ 82

PREFACE

The potential of technology to drive economic growth and solve pressing challenges is undeniable. In recent years, Africa has emerged as a frontier for technological innovation, particularly in areas such as mobile money, telemedicine, and agriculture. However, one area that holds immense, yet largely untapped potential, is machine learning. As a subset of artificial intelligence, machine learning offers the ability to analyze vast amounts of data, make predictions, and automate processes, all of which can be harnessed to drive progress across the continent.

The motivation for writing this book came from observing the incredible strides being made in various sectors in Africa through the application of machine learning. From improving access to financial services for the unbanked to enabling precision agriculture that helps smallholder farmers boost yields; machine learning is already playing a transformative role in African markets. Yet, despite these advancements, the broader potential of machine learning across the continent remains underexplored.

This book, "***Machine Learning in African Markets,***" is intended to bridge that gap by offering a comprehensive look at how machine learning is shaping key industries and what the future holds for its application in Africa. It is my hope that this book will serve as both an introduction to the possibilities of machine learning for readers unfamiliar with the technology and as a roadmap for businesses, policymakers, and innovators looking to leverage machine learning for development.

Throughout this book, you will find real-world examples of how machine learning is already being used to address some of Africa's most pressing challenges. You will also see a forward-looking analysis of the opportunities and challenges that lie ahead as machine learning becomes more integrated into African markets. It is my belief that with the right investments in education, infrastructure, and regulation, Africa can unlock the full potential of machine learning and become a global leader in artificial intelligence.

Thank you for taking the time to explore the fascinating world of machine learning and its potential in Africa. I hope that by the end of this book, you will be as excited about the future of machine learning in Africa as I am.

INTRODUCTION

Africa stands at a crossroads. On the one hand, the continent faces significant challenges, including limited access to healthcare, financial services, and education, as well as the growing threat of climate change. On the other hand, Africa is home to some of the world's fastest-growing economies, a youthful population eager to embrace new technologies, and an entrepreneurial spirit that is driving innovation across multiple sectors. It is within this context that machine learning has the potential to become a powerful catalyst for change.

Machine learning, a branch of artificial intelligence that enables computers to learn from data and make decisions without being explicitly programmed, is revolutionizing industries across the globe. In Africa, where access to infrastructure, skilled labor, and resources may be more limited than in other regions, machine learning offers the potential to overcome many of these barriers by providing efficient, data-driven solutions that can scale rapidly.

From agriculture to healthcare, finance, and energy, machine learning is beginning to make its mark in African markets. Farmers are using machine learning algorithms to optimize crop yields and predict weather patterns, while healthcare providers are using it to improve disease diagnosis and predict patient outcomes. In finance, machine learning enables fintech companies to extend credit to individuals who were previously excluded from the financial system, while in energy, it is helping optimize the distribution of renewable resources. These are just a few examples of how machine learning is already transforming industries across Africa.

But the potential for machine learning in Africa goes beyond individual industries. By enabling better decision-making, improving efficiency, and reducing costs, machine learning has the potential to drive economic growth, create jobs, and improve the quality of life for millions of people across the continent. It can help address some of Africa's most pressing challenges, such as improving food security, expanding access to healthcare, and building more resilient infrastructure in the face of climate change.

At the same time, the adoption of machine learning in Africa faces several challenges, including limited access to data, a shortage of skilled professionals, and the need for clear regulatory frameworks. As we explore these challenges throughout the book, it will become clear that while machine learning holds immense potential for Africa, realizing this potential will require collaboration between governments, businesses, educational institutions, and civil society.

This book is an invitation to explore the opportunities and challenges of machine learning in African markets. Whether you are a business leader looking to integrate machine learning into your operations, a policymaker considering how to regulate new technologies, or simply someone interested in the future of technology in Africa, this book will provide insights and examples that demonstrate the transformative power of machine learning on the continent.

The chapters that follow will dive deep into specific industries, explore real-world case studies, and offer a vision for the future of machine learning in Africa. As we embark on this journey together, I invite you to think not only about the potential of machine learning to solve the challenges we face today but also about how it can shape the Africa of tomorrow. Let's explore the future of machine learning in Africa.

1

Introduction To Machine Learning and African Markets

Machine learning has rapidly become one of the most influential and revolutionary technologies of our time, reshaping industries, transforming businesses, and fundamentally altering how individuals interact with technology. At its core, machine learning refers to the ability of computer systems to learn from data, identify patterns, and make decisions or predictions without being explicitly programmed to do so. This capability is derived from algorithms that improve automatically through experience, leveraging vast datasets to generate insights and solve complex problems.

The power of machine learning lies in its ability to adapt and evolve over time. Unlike traditional computer programs that rely on predefined rules, machine learning models become more efficient and accurate as they process more data. This technology has already started to disrupt key sectors, particularly in developed economies. However, the real potential of machine learning in less developed regions, especially in Africa, is only beginning to be explored. The African continent, with its diverse markets, rapidly expanding digital infrastructure, and young, dynamic population, represents a fertile ground for machine learning to drive significant innovation and growth.

Africa's economic landscape presents unique challenges and opportunities for machine learning. The continent is home to over a billion people, with economies at various stages of development. Major urban centers such as Lagos, Johannesburg, Nairobi, and Cairo are burgeoning hubs of commerce, finance, and technology, contributing to a vibrant and fast-growing digital economy. Yet, vast rural areas and less formalized economies, particularly in sectors like agriculture and retail, face challenges such as limited infrastructure, informal labor markets, and fragmented financial systems. These economic contrasts create both hurdles and opportunities for the application of machine learning.

One of the primary factors driving the relevance of machine learning in African markets is the continent's growing connectivity. The rapid penetration of mobile phones and the internet has made Africa one of the fastest-growing digital ecosystems in the world. More Africans are connected to mobile networks today than ever before, generating a wealth of digital data that was previously unavailable. From mobile money transactions and social media interactions to sensor data from farming operations, this surge in data opens the door for machine learning to provide insights and solutions tailored to the unique needs of African businesses and consumers.

Machine learning can be particularly transformative in sectors like agriculture, healthcare, and financial services. Agriculture, which remains the backbone of many African economies, faces numerous challenges, including climate variability, inefficient farming practices, and limited access to modern agricultural technologies. Machine learning can provide solutions by enabling farmers to make data-driven decisions. Predictive analytics, powered by machine learning, can forecast weather patterns, optimize irrigation schedules, and detect early signs of crop diseases, ultimately increasing yields and reducing waste. This is especially important for food security as Africa's population continues to grow rapidly, placing greater demand on agricultural systems.

In healthcare, the potential for machine learning is equally significant. Africa faces critical healthcare challenges, including shortages of medical professionals, limited access to healthcare infrastructure, and the ongoing burden of diseases such as malaria, tuberculosis, and HIV. Machine learning can assist healthcare providers by analyzing patient data, medical records, and diagnostic images to identify diseases more accurately and in less time. It can also predict disease outbreaks, enabling governments and healthcare organizations to allocate resources more effectively in advance of public health crises. Moreover, machine learning can support the development of personalized treatment plans, helping medical professionals provide better care in regions with limited resources.

In the financial services sector, machine learning is already driving the expansion of fintech solutions, which have become one of the most dynamic areas of innovation on the continent. Millions of Africans remain unbanked, with little access to formal financial services. Machine learning can analyze alternative data sources such as mobile phone usage, purchasing behaviors, and social media activity; to build credit profiles for individuals who lack traditional financial histories. This enables fintech companies to extend credit, microloans, and other financial products to underserved populations. By improving financial inclusion, machine learning has the potential to stimulate economic growth and empower individuals and small businesses across Africa.

Telecommunications, another rapidly growing sector in Africa, is also ripe for disruption by machine learning. With millions of mobile phone users generating enormous amounts of data every day, telecom providers can leverage machines learning to analyze customer behavior, optimize network performance, and enhance service delivery. Predictive models can anticipate demand for data services, helping telecom companies manage their networks more efficiently. Additionally, machine learning can improve customer engagement by enabling telecom providers to offer personalized pricing plans, promotions, and services that cater to the specific needs of their user base.

While the potential for machine learning in African markets is vast, there are significant challenges to its implementation. One of the biggest obstacles is the lack of reliable infrastructure in many parts of the continent. For machine learning systems to function optimally, they require access to large datasets and substantial computing power. In rural and underserved areas, limited access to high-speed internet, electricity, and computing resources can impede the deployment of machine learning technologies. Moreover, even in more developed urban centers, infrastructure bottlenecks such as inconsistent power supply and underdeveloped data centers remain common.

Another challenge is the availability of skilled professionals. While Africa has a rapidly growing pool of tech-savvy youth, there is still a significant gap when it comes to the specialized knowledge required to develop and deploy machine learning solutions. Data scientists, machine learning engineers, and AI specialists are in short supply globally, and Africa is no exception. Without this talent, businesses and governments across the continent will struggle to fully harness the power of machine learning. Bridging this skills gap will require coordinated efforts from educational institutions, governments, and private enterprises to invest in training programs, scholarships, and mentorship opportunities that build capacity in machine learning and data science.

In addition to infrastructure and talent, the success of machine learning in Africa will depend on collaboration between key stakeholders, including governments, businesses, and educational institutions. Governments have a crucial role to play in creating regulatory frameworks that foster innovation while ensuring that data is used responsibly and ethically. They must also invest in digital infrastructure to support the widespread adoption of machine learning technologies. Businesses, particularly those in the tech sector, can lead the way by developing machine learning solutions tailored to local needs and by partnering with governments and educational institutions to drive skills development. Meanwhile, universities and training centers across Africa must continue to offer courses and research programs that prepare the next generation of machine learning experts.

Moreover, there is a need for African countries to establish strong data governance policies. The widespread use of machine learning involves collecting and processing vast amounts of personal and commercial data. Without adequate data privacy regulations, there is a risk of misuse, exploitation, or even exclusion, particularly when it comes to credit scoring or healthcare applications. Governments and regulatory bodies need to strike a balance between enabling data-driven innovation and protecting the rights and privacy of individuals. Transparent, ethical, and equitable use of data will be key to building trust and ensuring the long-term sustainability of machine learning technologies across the continent.

Despite these challenges, the opportunities for machine learning in Africa are immense. As the continent continues to embrace digital transformation, machine learning will play a pivotal role in shaping Africa's future. By providing innovative solutions to some of the continent's most pressing challenges. From improving agricultural productivity and food security to expanding access to financial services and healthcare, machine learning has the potential to drive economic growth, reduce poverty, and enhance the overall quality of life for millions of people.

In conclusion, while the road ahead may be complex, the potential rewards are substantial. Machine learning is not a silver bullet, but it is a powerful tool that, when applied effectively, can accelerate development across a wide range of industries. As we delve deeper into the specific applications of machine learning in subsequent chapters, we will explore how different sectors are already benefiting from this technology, the challenges they face, and the steps needed to ensure that Africa fully harnesses the power of machine learning to drive growth and innovation across the continent.

2

Opportunities for Machine Learning in Africa

Africa, with its diverse economies, rapidly growing population, and evolving digital landscape, presents immense opportunities for the application of machine learning. While much of the global discourse surrounding machine learning has focused on its potential in developed regions, the transformative potential of this technology in African markets is just as significant, if not more so. The continent's unique challenges, coupled with the increasing availability of data and technological infrastructure, create an ideal environment for innovation powered by machine learning. From agriculture to healthcare, finance, education, and more, machine learning offers the possibility to unlock new avenues of development, drive economic growth, and address persistent challenges.

One of the most promising sectors for machine learning in Africa is agriculture. Agriculture remains the backbone of many African economies, providing livelihoods for a substantial portion of the population. Despite its importance, the sector faces numerous challenges, including resource inefficiency, unpredictable weather patterns exacerbated by climate change, and limited access to modern farming techniques. Machine learning offers a suite of tools that can help farmers overcome these challenges by enabling them to make data-driven decisions.

For instance, machine learning models can be used to predict weather patterns with greater accuracy, helping farmers plan planting and harvesting schedules more effectively. Furthermore, predictive analytics can forecast crop yields and detect early signs of crop diseases, giving farmers critical insights that allow them to respond proactively. These insights can improve productivity, reduce waste, and ultimately lead to greater food security across the continent. In regions prone to drought, machine learning models can also optimize irrigation schedules, ensuring that water resources are used efficiently and sustainably. This is particularly important as many African countries face water scarcity, which has a direct impact on agricultural output.

Another area where machine learning holds great promise is in financial services. Africa has long struggled with financial inclusion, as millions of people across the continent lack access to formal banking services. This financial exclusion limits economic opportunities, stifling growth and leaving many people reliant on informal, often exploitative financial arrangements. The rise of fintech in Africa, driven by mobile money and digital financial services, has begun to address this issue, and machine learning is playing an increasingly important role in expanding financial inclusion.

Machine learning algorithms can analyze vast amounts of data to assess creditworthiness, even for individuals without traditional credit histories. By leveraging alternative data sources such as mobile phone usage, purchasing behaviors, and social media activity, machine learning models can create more accurate credit profiles for underserved populations. This allows financial institutions to extend loans, microcredit, and other financial products to a broader range of customers, including smallholder farmers, informal traders, and others who have been excluded from the formal financial system. In addition to improving access to credit, machine learning can also be used to detect and prevent fraud, ensuring the security of digital financial services and building trust among users.

Healthcare is another sector where machine learning has the potential to revolutionize service delivery in Africa. The continent faces significant healthcare challenges, including a shortage of medical professionals, limited access to healthcare facilities, and a high burden of infectious diseases such as malaria, tuberculosis, and HIV. These challenges are further compounded by emerging threats, such as non-communicable diseases and the impact of climate change on public health. Machine learning can assist healthcare providers in diagnosing diseases, predicting outbreaks, and personalizing treatment plans.

For example, machine learning-powered diagnostic tools can analyze medical images to identify signs of diseases such as tuberculosis, cancer, and pneumonia. This can be especially valuable in rural areas where access to radiologists and specialists is limited. By automating the diagnostic process, machine learning can reduce the need for specialized human intervention, improving the speed and accuracy of diagnoses. In addition, machine learning models can analyze electronic health records and other patient data to predict the likelihood of disease outbreaks, enabling healthcare systems to respond more effectively to public health emergencies.

Moreover, machine learning can help optimize the allocation of scarce medical resources. In many African countries, healthcare infrastructure is strained, and resources such as hospital beds, medical equipment, and pharmaceuticals are limited. Machine learning can help optimize these resources by predicting patient demand, identifying gaps in service delivery, and recommending strategies for improving efficiency. This can lead to better outcomes for patients and help healthcare systems function more effectively, even in resource-constrained environments.

The telecommunications industry, which has seen explosive growth across the continent due to the widespread adoption of mobile phones, is another area where machine learning is having a significant impact. With the increasing penetration of smartphones and internet access, telecom companies are collecting vast amounts of data on user behavior. Machine learning can help these companies analyze this data to improve network performance, optimize pricing models, and offer personalized services to customers. By leveraging machine learning, telecom providers can enhance customer satisfaction, increase revenue, and support the continent's growing digital economy.

For instance, predictive analytics can help telecom companies anticipate periods of high network demand and adjust their operations accordingly. Machine learning models can also analyze customer usage patterns to identify opportunities for upselling and cross-selling services, such as data bundles, streaming services, and mobile banking products. Furthermore, machine learning can be used to detect and resolve network issues in real time, ensuring that customers experience fewer disruptions and enjoy a higher quality of service.

In addition to sector-specific opportunities, machine learning can also contribute to solving broader challenges that cut across multiple industries. One such challenge is infrastructure development. Many African countries still lack adequate infrastructure, particularly in rural areas. Machine learning can help optimize infrastructure projects by analyzing data on population growth, urbanization trends, and resource availability. This can lead to smarter decisions about where to build roads, schools, hospitals, and other critical infrastructure.

Similarly, machine learning can play a role in improving energy access across the continent. By analyzing data from renewable energy sources such as solar and wind, machine learning models can help optimize energy distribution and reduce reliance on fossil fuels. This is particularly important as many African countries seek to expand access to electricity while reducing their carbon footprint. Machine learning can help ensure that energy resources are used efficiently, making renewable energy systems more reliable and cost-effective.

Education is another critical area where machine learning can unlock new opportunities for Africa. As the continent's population continues to grow, there is a pressing need to provide quality education for millions of young people. Machine learning can help personalize education, tailoring learning experiences to individual students' needs and abilities. This is particularly valuable in regions where access to teachers and educational resources is limited. For example, machine learning models can analyze student performance data to identify areas where additional support is needed, allowing educators to provide targeted interventions.

Additionally, machine learning can help identify gaps in the education system and recommend strategies for improving learning outcomes. By analyzing data on school performance, teacher effectiveness, and student achievement, machine learning can provide insights that help policymakers make more informed decisions about resource allocation and curriculum development. By leveraging machine learning, African countries can build more resilient and inclusive education systems that prepare young people for the jobs of the future.

Entrepreneurship and innovation are also set to benefit from machine learning in Africa. The continent has a vibrant entrepreneurial ecosystem, with startups emerging in sectors such as fintech, e-commerce, healthtech, and agritech. Machine learning can help these startups develop innovative products and services that address local needs. For example, machine learning can be used to analyze market trends, predict customer behavior, and optimize pricing strategies. By incorporating machine learning into their operations, African entrepreneurs can gain a competitive edge, scale their businesses more efficiently, and attract investment from both local and international sources.

Governments across Africa are also recognizing the potential of machine learning to drive economic growth and development. By leveraging data and machine learning models, policymakers can make more informed decisions about resource allocation, economic planning, and public services. For example, machine learning can be used to predict economic trends, assess the impact of policy changes, and identify areas where government intervention is most needed. In addition, machine learning can help governments improve public service delivery by automating administrative tasks, reducing bureaucracy, and enhancing transparency.

Despite the many opportunities that machine learning presents for Africa, there are challenges that must be addressed to fully realize its potential. One major challenge is the availability of high-quality data. While mobile phones and internet access have improved data collection, there are still gaps in data availability, particularly in rural areas. Ensuring that machine learning models are trained in accurate and representative data is critical to their success.

Additionally, there is a need for greater investment in technological infrastructure, such as data centers and high-speed internet, to support the deployment of machine learning solutions across the continent. Furthermore, the success of machine learning in Africa will depend on the availability of skilled professionals. While Africa has a growing pool of tech talent, there is a shortage of professionals with expertise in machine learning and data science. Governments, educational institutions, and the private sector must collaborate to create training programs and educational opportunities that equip young people with the skills they need to thrive in the digital economy.

In conclusion, the opportunities for machine learning in Africa are vast and varied. From agriculture to healthcare, finance, education, and beyond, machine learning has the potential to transform industries, drive economic growth, and improve the quality of life for millions of people across the continent. By addressing challenges such as data availability, infrastructure, and skills development, Africa can harness the power of machine learning to create a brighter, more prosperous future.

3

Challenges Facing Machine Learning in African Markets

While the opportunities for machine learning in Africa are vast, they come with a series of challenges that must be addressed to fully realize the potential of this transformative technology. Africa is a continent of immense diversity, with over 50 countries, each with its own set of economic conditions, infrastructure levels, governance structures, and cultural dynamics. These factors present unique obstacles to the widespread adoption and implementation of machine learning technologies across the continent. From infrastructure limitations and data scarcity to regulatory hurdles and a shortage of skilled talent, overcoming these challenges is essential for machine learning to thrive in African markets.

One of the primary challenges is the lack of adequate infrastructure. Machine learning requires robust technological infrastructure, including access to high-speed internet, reliable electricity, and data centers capable of processing and storing large volumes of data. In many African countries, particularly in rural areas, this infrastructure is either limited or nonexistent. Power outages, poor internet connectivity, and insufficient digital infrastructure are common issues that can hinder the deployment of machine learning solutions. For example, machine learning models need continuous access to data and computational resources to function effectively, and any interruption in these resources can impact the performance of these models.

In rural areas, where much of Africa's population resides, the challenge of infrastructure is particularly acute. Limited access to electricity and internet services makes it difficult for machine learning solutions to reach their full potential. This is a critical issue for sectors such as agriculture, where many smallholder farmers could benefit from machine learning technologies but are unable to access them due to infrastructural constraints. While urban centers like Lagos, Nairobi, and Johannesburg may have the necessary infrastructure in place, the digital divide between urban and rural areas remains a significant barrier to the widespread adoption of machine learning across the continent.

Another major challenge is the scarcity of reliable and high-quality data. Machine learning models rely heavily on large datasets to train algorithms and make accurate predictions. However, in many African markets, data collection is inconsistent, incomplete, or outdated. This is especially true in sectors such as healthcare, agriculture, and education, where much of the data is collected manually or not collected at all. For example, farmers in rural areas may not have access to tools or platforms that allow them to track their crop yields, soil conditions, or weather patterns. Similarly, healthcare providers in underserved regions may not have the resources to digitize patient records, making it difficult to leverage machine learning for disease diagnosis and treatment.

The issue of data fragmentation further complicates the situation. In many cases, data is stolen within individual organizations or government agencies, preventing the creation of comprehensive datasets that are critical for machine learning models to provide accurate insights. This fragmentation is often due to a lack of data-sharing frameworks and policies that facilitate collaboration between stakeholders. For example, data on transportation systems, public health, or financial transactions may be spread across different government departments or private companies, making it difficult to build holistic machine learning models that address challenges on a broader scale. In the absence of integrated data systems, machine learning applications may yield biased or incomplete results, which can limit their effectiveness.

Beyond infrastructure and data challenges, there is also a significant skills gap in the field of machine learning and artificial intelligence (AI) across Africa. While the continent has a growing pool of tech-savvy young people, there is still a shortage of professionals with the specialized knowledge required to develop and deploy machine learning solutions. Data scientists, machine learning engineers, and AI specialists are in high demand globally, and Africa is no exception. Educational institutions across the continent are only beginning to offer programs focused on machine learning, data science, and AI, but the current capacity is insufficient to meet the demand for skilled professionals.

This skills gap poses a significant challenge for African businesses and governments seeking to adopt machine learning technologies. Without a skilled workforce capable of designing, implementing, and maintaining machine learning models, the continent risks falling behind in the global race to harness AI-driven innovation. Addressing this challenge will require coordinated efforts between governments, educational institutions, and the private sector to invest in education and training programs that build capacity in machine learning and data science. Initiatives such as coding boot camps, mentorship programs, and scholarships for data science degrees are already underway in some countries, but more needs to be done to scale these efforts across the continent.

Regulatory and policy challenges also play a role in slowing the adoption of machine learning in African markets. Many African governments are still grappling with how to regulate emerging technologies such as artificial intelligence and machine learning. In some cases, there is a lack of clear guidelines and frameworks for how businesses and organizations should use machine learning, particularly when it comes to issues like data privacy, ethical considerations, and the potential impact on jobs. Regulatory uncertainty can create an environment where businesses are hesitant to invest in machine learning initiatives for fear of running afoul of government regulations.

Data privacy is a particularly important issue. Machine learning models often require access to vast amounts of personal and sensitive data, such as financial records, health information, and social media activity. Without adequate data protection regulations, there is a risk of misuse or exploitation of this data, which could harm individuals and erode trust in machine learning technologies. Several African countries, including South Africa, Kenya, and Nigeria, have enacted data protection laws in recent years, but the enforcement of these laws remains inconsistent. Ensuring that data privacy regulations are robust, transparent, and enforced will be critical to fostering trust in machine learning systems and encouraging their adoption.

Ethical considerations also come into play when deploying machine learning in African markets. Machine learning models can inadvertently reinforce existing biases if they are trained on biased datasets. For example, a machine learning model used to assess creditworthiness could disproportionately disadvantage certain demographic groups if the data used to train the model reflects historical inequalities in access to financial services. Ensuring that machine learning systems are fair, transparent, and accountable is essential to preventing discrimination and ensuring that these technologies benefit all segments of society.

The impact of automation on jobs is another area of concern. While machine learning has the potential to improve efficiency and productivity across various sectors, there is also a fear that automation could lead to job displacement, particularly in industries that rely heavily on manual labor. In Africa, where unemployment and underemployment are already significant challenges, the potential for job losses due to automation is a source of anxiety for workers and policymakers alike. To address this issue, governments and businesses must work together to create strategies that balance the benefits of automation with the need to protect workers and create new job opportunities in the digital economy. Cultural and societal factors can also present challenges to the adoption of machine learning in African markets. In some cases, there may be a lack of awareness or understanding of what machine learning is and how it can be applied to solve local problems. This lack of awareness can lead to resistance to adopting new technologies, particularly in industries that have traditionally relied on manual labor and face-to-face interactions. Building trust and demonstrating the tangible benefits of machine learning will be crucial in overcoming these societal barriers. Engaging with community leaders, industry stakeholders, and the public through educational campaigns and pilot projects can showcase the positive impact of machine learning and create a sense of ownership and empowerment.

Despite these challenges, there are solutions that can help address the obstacles facing machine learning in Africa. One such solution is increased investment in infrastructure development. Governments and private enterprises can work together to improve internet connectivity, expand access to reliable electricity, and build data centers that can support machine learning initiatives. By creating the necessary infrastructure, African countries can ensure that machine learning technologies have the foundation they need to thrive.

On the regulatory front, African governments can take steps to create clear and transparent policies that support the ethical and responsible use of machine learning. Establishing frameworks that protect data privacy, promote transparency, and ensure that machine learning technologies are used for the benefit of society will be key. Additionally, governments can engage with international organizations and experts in AI and machine learning to develop the best practices and avoid common pitfalls in regulating emerging technologies.

Finally, raising awareness and building trust within local communities will be essential to the successful adoption of machine learning in Africa. Demonstrating how machine learning can improve lives, whether through better healthcare, more efficient farming practices, or improved financial inclusion can help dispel fears about automation and build enthusiasm for the technology. Engaging with community leaders, industry stakeholders, and the general public through educational campaigns and pilot projects can showcase the positive impact of machine learning and create a sense of ownership and empowerment.

In conclusion, while the challenges facing machine learning in African markets are significant, they are not insurmountable. By addressing issues related to infrastructure, data availability, talent development, regulation, and societal acceptance, Africa can unlock the full potential of machine learning and position itself as a leader in AI-driven innovation. The next chapters will explore how specific sectors are navigating these challenges and how machine learning is already beginning to make a difference in African markets.

4

Data Availability and Quality in Africa

Data is the foundation upon which machine learning systems are built. Without access to large amounts of high-quality data, machine learning models cannot effectively analyze information, recognize patterns, or make accurate predictions. In regions like Africa, where digital ecosystems are still developing, the availability and quality of data are critical issues that can either enable or hinder the adoption of machine learning technologies.

While Africa has made significant strides in improving access to digital platforms, especially through the widespread adoption of mobile phones, there are still considerable challenges when it comes to collecting, storing, and managing data. Many sectors, particularly in agriculture, healthcare, and education, still rely on manual data collection methods, which can result in incomplete, inconsistent, or inaccurate data. Furthermore, a lack of standardization and integration across industries leads to data fragmentation, preventing the creation of comprehensive datasets that can support sophisticated machine learning applications.

Machine learning models are only as good as the data they are trained on. The success of these models depends on having access to diverse, accurate, and representative datasets that reflect the complexity of real-world conditions. For example, in agriculture, machine learning algorithms can help predict crop yields, optimize planting schedules, and monitor soil health but only if they have access to reliable data on weather patterns, soil composition, and historical crop performance. Similarly, in healthcare, machine learning models can assist in diagnosing diseases and recommending treatments, but they require access to accurate patient records, diagnostic results, and population health data to function effectively.

The challenge in many African markets is that such high-quality, structured data is often hard to come by. Many African countries lack the infrastructure necessary to collect and manage data systematically, particularly in rural areas. In sectors such as agriculture, much of the data is still gathered manually by individual farmers, with little to no digital record-keeping. This creates gaps in the data that machine learning models rely on for training, leading to inaccurate or incomplete predictions. In healthcare, many hospitals and clinics, particularly those in underserved regions, still use paper records, making it difficult to digitize patient information and feed it into machine learning systems.

Data fragmentation is a major barrier to implementing machine learning at scale in Africa. Data is often siloed within different organizations, sectors, or government agencies, limiting the ability of machine learning systems to access the comprehensive, cross-sectoral information needed for accurate modeling. For example, transportation data might be controlled by municipal agencies, while data on healthcare, education, and public services is held by separate entities. Without mechanisms for sharing data across these silos, machine learning models may only have access to partial datasets, limiting their effectiveness.

This fragmentation is particularly problematic in areas such as urban planning and infrastructure development, where data from multiple sources such as population density, transportation networks, and land use must be combined to create accurate models. For example, if a city wants to use machine learning to predict traffic patterns and optimize transportation routes, it will need access to data from various sources, including vehicle traffic data, public transport schedules, and pedestrian movement patterns. However, if these datasets are fragmented across different departments and agencies, the machine learning models will not have the full picture, leading to suboptimal predictions.

In addition to the lack of data-sharing frameworks, there are also issues related to data quality and reliability. Even when data is available, it may not be sufficiently accurate, up-to-date, or comprehensive to support machine learning applications. This can result in models that produce biased or inaccurate results, especially if the data is skewed towards certain regions or populations. In healthcare, for instance, a machine learning model trained on data from urban hospitals may not be applicable to rural areas, where the health challenges and access to medical services are different.

The collection of high-quality data is a significant challenge in many parts of Africa, particularly in rural and underserved areas. In agriculture, for example, data on crop yields, weather conditions, and soil health is often collected manually by farmers, who may lack the tools or knowledge to accurately record this information. This leads to inconsistencies in the data, which can make it difficult to build reliable machine learning models. Additionally, many farmers operate in informal markets, where transactions and production data are not systematically tracked, and there are further complicating efforts to collect accurate information.

In healthcare, the situation is similar. While some urban hospitals and clinics have adopted electronic health records (EHR) systems, many healthcare providers in rural areas still rely on paper-based systems, which are prone to errors and difficult to digitize. Without accurate and comprehensive patient data, it becomes challenging to develop machine learning models that can predict disease outbreaks, recommend treatments, or optimize healthcare resource allocation. Furthermore, there is often a lack of data on social determinants of health, such as access to clean water, sanitation, and education, which are critical for understanding the broader context of health outcomes in African populations.

Even in sectors such as education, where digital platforms are increasingly being used, data collection can be fragmented and inconsistent. Schools may collect data on student attendance, performance, and learning outcomes, but this data is often not standardized or shared across regions, making it difficult to build comprehensive models that can provide insights at a national or continental level. This lack of standardization can lead to disparities in education quality and outcomes, particularly in rural and underserved areas where access to technology is limited.

Addressing the challenges of data availability and quality in Africa will require coordinated efforts from governments, businesses, and international organizations. Several solutions can help overcome these barriers and enable the widespread adoption of machine learning across the continent.

One of the most critical steps is investing in the digital infrastructure needed to support data collection, storage, and analysis. This includes expanding access to high-speed internet, particularly in rural areas, and building data centers that can process and store large volumes of information. By improving digital infrastructure, African countries can ensure that data is collected more efficiently and made available for machine learning applications.

Governments and businesses should work together to create data-sharing frameworks that facilitate collaboration between different sectors and organizations. This could involve developing open data platforms where public and private entities can share datasets in a standardized format. Such platforms would enable machine learning models to access a broader range of data, improving their accuracy and relevance. For example, transportation, healthcare, and education data could be shared to create more comprehensive models for urban planning and social services. To improve the quality and consistency of data, there is a need for standardization in how data is collected across sectors. This could involve developing guidelines for collecting and reporting data on agriculture, healthcare, education, and other key areas. By standardizing data collection practices, African countries can ensure that machine learning models are trained on accurate and comparable datasets, leading to better outcomes.

Addressing the data challenge will also require building the capacity of local institutions and professionals to collect, manage, and analyze data effectively. This could involve providing training to farmers, healthcare workers, teachers, and other stakeholders on how to use digital tools for data collection. Governments and educational institutions should also invest in developing a workforce skilled in data science and machine learning, who can design and implement data-driven solutions tailored to local needs. Encouraging the use of open data can also help improve data availability and quality in Africa. Several initiatives, such as the African Open Data Network, are working to promote the use of open data for development. By making datasets publicly available, governments and organizations can encourage innovation and enable researchers, entrepreneurs, and policymakers to use machine learning to solve pressing challenges. Open data can also help reduce duplication of efforts, as multiple stakeholders can collaborate and build upon shared datasets.

International partnerships can play a key role in addressing the data challenges facing Africa. Many global organizations, including the United Nations, the World Bank, and various NGOs, are working to improve data collection and management in Africa. These organizations can provide technical expertise, funding, and resources to help African countries build the infrastructure and systems needed to support data-driven development. Partnerships between African governments and international tech companies, such as Google, Microsoft, and IBM, can also help accelerate the adoption of machine learning by providing access to advanced technologies and data analytics platforms.

In addition to providing resources, international partnerships can also help African countries learn from best practices in data management and governance. For example, countries in Europe and North America have developed robust data protection regulations, such as the General Data Protection Regulation (GDPR) in the European Union. By collaborating with international partners, African countries can adopt similar frameworks to ensure that data is collected, stored, and used in a way that protects privacy, and fosters trust in machine learning systems.

Data is the lifeblood of machine learning, and addressing the challenges of data availability and quality in Africa is critical to unlocking the full potential of this technology. While there are significant barriers, including fragmented datasets, inconsistent data collection practices, and a lack of digital infrastructure, there are also promising solutions on the horizon. By investing in infrastructure, developing data-sharing frameworks, standardizing data collection, and building local capacity, Africa can create the conditions needed for machine learning to thrive. International partnerships will also play a crucial role in supporting these efforts, ensuring that Africa can harness the power of data to drive innovation and development across the continent.

5

Machine Learning for Financial Inclusion in Africa

Financial inclusion remains one of Africa's most pressing challenges, with millions of people across the continent still lacking access to formal banking services. This exclusion limits economic opportunities for individuals, small businesses, and communities, making it difficult for many Africans to save, borrow, or invest in their futures. Traditional banking services remain out of reach for much of the population, especially in rural areas, due to the high cost of banking infrastructure, the lack of formal identification systems, and the absence of formal credit histories. However, the rise of digital financial services especially mobile money has begun to bridge this gap, providing millions of unbanked and underbanked Africans with access to basic financial services. Machine learning has the potential to further accelerate this trend, driving financial inclusion by offering innovative solutions that extend credit, detect fraud, assess risk, and streamline service delivery for underserved populations.

One of the most significant barriers to financial inclusion in Africa is the lack of access to credit. Traditional lending models rely on credit histories, but many Africans do not have access to formal financial systems that generate such records. This makes it difficult for banks and lending institutions to assess the creditworthiness of potential borrowers, particularly those who live in rural areas or work in the informal economy. Machine learning offers a powerful solution to this problem by enabling lenders to use alternative data sources to assess credit risk. By analyzing non-traditional data points such as mobile phone usage, payment history on utility bills, social media activity, and transaction patterns; machine learning models can build a comprehensive profile of a borrower's financial reliability. This allows fintech companies and microfinance institutions to extend loans to individuals who would otherwise be considered too risky by traditional standards.

In Kenya and Tanzania, for example, companies like Tala and Branch are using machine learning algorithms to assess creditworthiness and offer microloans to consumers who have limited or no access to traditional banking services. These fintech platforms analyze data from mobile phones—such as call patterns, SMS history, and mobile money transactions—to determine the likelihood that a borrower will repay a loan. This enables them to make lending decisions within minutes, providing fast, flexible access to credit for individuals and small businesses. For many borrowers, especially those in rural areas, this is their first opportunity to access formal credit, which can be used to invest in small businesses, pay school fees, or cover emergency expenses.

The ability of machine learning to use alternative data for credit scoring is a game changer, particularly in regions where many people operate outside of the formal financial system. By leveraging data from everyday activities such as phone usage or purchasing habits. Machine learning opens the door to financial inclusion for millions of Africans who have historically been excluded from formal lending. This approach not only allows lenders to extend credit to a broader population but also reduces the reliance on traditional credit scoring methods, which can be inaccessible or irrelevant for much of the continent's population.

In addition to expanding access to credit, machine learning is helping financial institutions offer more personalized services to African consumers. By analyzing transaction data and customer behavior, machine learning models can identify patterns and predict future needs, enabling financial service providers to tailor products and services to individual users. This level of personalization is particularly valuable in markets where consumers may have limited financial literacy and may not fully understand the range of services available to them. For example, machine learning can help financial institutions develop savings plans that are aligned with a user's income patterns and financial goals. A fintech platform might analyze a user's spending habits and recommend a savings plan that encourages them to set aside small amounts of money at regular intervals, based on their predicted cash flow. Similarly, machine learning can help users manage their budgets more effectively by providing personalized financial advice, such as alerting them when they are overspending or suggesting ways to reduce expenses.

One of the most important contributions of machine learning in the financial sector is its ability to detect fraud and manage risks. As digital financial services expand across Africa, the risk of fraud and cybercrime grows. Machine learning algorithms are capable of analyzing vast amounts of transactional data in real-time to detect anomalies and flag suspicious activities. These systems can identify unusual spending patterns, such as multiple transactions from different geographic locations in a short period of time, which may indicate fraud. Machine learning models can also learn from historical fraud data, allowing them to detect new types of fraud as they emerge. This ability to continuously adapt and improve makes machine learning a valuable tool in the fight against financial crime.

Mobile money platforms like M-Pesa in Kenya have implemented machine learning systems to monitor transactions and detect fraudulent activities in real time. By leveraging data from millions of daily transactions, these platforms can identify unusual patterns that may indicate fraudulent behavior, such as unauthorized account access or suspicious transfers. This helps to reduce the incidence of fraud, providing a safer and more secure experience for users. The use of machine learning for fraud detection not only protects consumers but also builds trust in digital financial services, encouraging more people to adopt these platforms.

Machine learning is also playing a key role in improving financial literacy across Africa. Many Africans are not fully familiar with formal financial services or how to manage their money effectively, particularly those who are new to digital financial platforms. Machine learning-powered financial education tools can provide personalized learning experiences that help users understand important financial concepts, such as budgeting, saving, investing, and managing debt. By analyzing user behavior, financial apps can offer customized advice based on an individual's financial situation. For example, a machine learning-powered app might suggest specific budgeting strategies based on a user's spending habits or provide tips on how to improve their creditworthiness. These personalized recommendations can help users make more informed financial decisions, improving their financial well-being and promoting greater financial inclusion.

The impact of machine learning extends beyond individuals to small and medium-sized enterprises (SMEs), which are the backbone of many African economies. SMEs often face significant challenges when trying to access financing, as they may lack the financial records required by traditional lenders. Machine learning can help solve this problem by enabling financial institutions to assess the creditworthiness of SMEs based on alternative data sources. For example, machine learning algorithms can analyze a company's transaction history, customer reviews, and supplier relationships to create a more comprehensive picture of the business's financial health. This allows lenders to offer more favorable lending terms to SMEs, providing them with the capital they need to grow and create jobs.

In addition to improving access to credit, machine learning can help SMEs optimize their financial management. By analyzing cash flow data and other financial metrics, machine learning models can provide businesses with insights into their operations, helping them forecast demand, manage inventory, and allocate resources more effectively. This can be especially valuable for businesses that operate in volatile markets or face unpredictable cash flow patterns. By providing SMEs with the tools, they need to manage their finances more effectively, machine learning can help them become more resilient and competitive.

Despite the significant potential of machine learning to drive financial inclusion in Africa, there are challenges that must be addressed to ensure its successful implementation. One of the key challenges is the availability of high-quality data. While mobile money and digital financial services have generated a wealth of data, much of Africa's economy remains cash-based, particularly in rural areas. This makes it difficult for machine learning models to gather the data they need to make accurate predictions. Governments and financial institutions must work together to digitize financial transactions and promote the use of digital payments in underserved areas.

Another challenge is the need for robust regulatory frameworks to ensure that machine learning is used responsibly in financial services. As machine learning becomes more integrated into the financial sector, regulators must create clear guidelines for data privacy and consumer protection. It is essential to ensure that machine learning systems do not reinforce existing biases or create new forms of discrimination, particularly when it comes to credit scoring and lending decisions. Policymakers must work with industry stakeholders to develop ethical standards for the use of machine learning in financial services, ensuring that it is used in a way that benefits all consumers, regardless of their socio-economic background.

In conclusion, machine learning has the potential to transform financial services in Africa by expanding access to credit, improving the delivery of personalized financial products, detecting fraud, and promoting financial literacy. By leveraging alternative data sources and predictive analytics, machine learning can provide innovative solutions to some of the continent's most pressing financial challenges. While there are hurdles to overcome, the opportunities for machine learning to drive financial inclusion and economic empowerment across Africa are immense. As digital financial services continue to grow, machine learning will play an increasingly important role in shaping the future of finance on the continent, helping to create a more inclusive and equitable financial ecosystem.

6

Agriculture and Machine Learning: Feeding the Continent

Agriculture is the backbone of many African economies, serving as the primary source of livelihood for a significant portion of the population and playing a critical role in ensuring food security. Despite its importance, Africa's agricultural sector faces several challenges that threaten its productivity and sustainability. Climate change, resource inefficiencies, pest infestations, and limited access to modern farming techniques are just a few of the issues that farmers across the continent grapple with on a daily basis. However, machine learning offers a powerful solution to many of these challenges by providing data-driven insights that can transform the way agriculture is practiced. By leveraging machine learning technologies, farmers can optimize crop yields, reduce waste, and make more informed decisions about everything from resource allocation to market trends.

One of the most promising applications of machine learning in African agriculture is crop yield prediction. Accurately predicting how much a farmer can expect to harvest in a given season can have a profound impact on how resources are allocated, how planting and harvesting are timed, and how farmers prepare for potential shortages or surpluses. Machine learning models can analyze vast amounts of data on historical crop performance, soil health, weather patterns, and market conditions to generate accurate crop yield predictions. This is particularly important in regions where farmers rely on rain-fed agriculture, as unpredictable weather patterns due to climate change can lead to significant fluctuations in crop yields. By providing farmers with more reliable yield forecasts, machine learning enables them to plan more effectively, avoid overproduction, and make better decisions about which crops to plant based on current market demand.

Precision farming, which refers to the use of technology and data to optimize farming practices, is another area where machine learning is beginning to have a significant impact. Traditional farming practices often involve applying water, fertilizer, and pesticides uniformly across entire fields, regardless of varying conditions. This can lead to waste, inefficiency, and environmental damage. Machine learning models can analyze data from sensors placed in the soil or on crops to monitor critical factors such as moisture levels, nutrient content, and pest activity in real-time. Based on this data, the models can recommend precise amounts of water or fertilizer to apply, ensuring that each part of the field receives the exact amount it needs to thrive. Precision farming not only increases crop yields but also helps farmers conserve valuable resources, such as water and fertilizers, which are often in short supply in many African regions.

Pest and disease management is another critical area where machine learning can play a transformative role. Pests and diseases can have devastating effects on agricultural productivity, leading to massive crop losses and economic hardship for farmers. Machine learning algorithms can analyze data on pest populations, weather conditions, and crop health to predict when and where pest outbreaks are likely to occur. For example, satellite imagery combined with machine learning can be used to detect early signs of pest infestations, allowing farmers to intervene before the pests spread and cause significant damage. Additionally, machine learning models can help farmers diagnose crop diseases by analyzing images of affected plants and recommending appropriate treatments. This level of precision in disease management can significantly reduce the economic losses associated with pests and diseases while helping farmers adopt more sustainable pest control practices.

Climate change is an increasingly pressing concern for African agriculture, as the continent is highly vulnerable to extreme weather events such as droughts, floods, and heatwaves. These events can disrupt farming activities, reduce crop yields, and threaten food security across the continent. Machine learning has the potential to help farmers adapt to the challenges posed by climate change by providing early warnings of extreme weather events and recommending strategies for mitigating their impact. For example, machine learning models can analyze historical weather data to predict the likelihood of a drought occurring in a particular region and recommend drought-resistant crop varieties that are better suited to the changing climate. By helping farmers prepare for and adapt to the effects of climate change, machine learning can play a crucial role in ensuring the long-term sustainability of African agriculture.

Market analysis is another important application of machine learning in agriculture. Many African farmers struggle to sell their produce at fair prices, often due to a lack of access to reliable market information. Without knowledge of current market trends, consumer demand, and price fluctuations, farmers are often forced to sell their crops at a loss or rely on middlemen who take a significant portion of the profits. Machine learning models can analyze data on market prices, supply and demand trends, and consumer preferences to provide farmers with real-time insights into the best times and places to sell their produce. By connecting farmers directly with buyers and reducing their reliance on intermediaries, machine learning can help farmers improve their market access, maximize their profits, and ensure that they receive fair compensation for their hard work.

In addition to improving crop yields, resource efficiency, and market access, machine learning can also support efforts to combat food insecurity by enabling more effective food distribution. In many African countries, food shortages are not necessarily caused by a lack of agricultural production but by inefficiencies in the supply chain. Machine learning can help address these inefficiencies by optimizing food distribution networks, predicting supply chain disruptions, and ensuring that food reaches the areas where it is needed most. By improving the efficiency and reliability of food supply chains, machine learning can help reduce food waste, lower transportation costs, and ensure that food is distributed more equitably across the continent.

Despite its vast potential, there are challenges that must be addressed to fully realize the benefits of machine learning in African agriculture. One of the most significant challenges is the lack of digital infrastructure, particularly in rural areas where many farmers live and work. Access to reliable internet, electricity, and digital tools is essential for the successful implementation of machine learning technologies, but these resources are often in short supply in many parts of the continent. Additionally, there is a need for greater investment in training and capacity-building to ensure that farmers and agricultural professionals have the skills and knowledge needed to effectively use machine learning tools. Governments, development organizations, and the private sector must work together to address these infrastructure and capacity challenges, ensuring that the benefits of machine learning are accessible to all farmers, regardless of their location or resources.

In conclusion, machine learning has the potential to revolutionize agriculture in Africa by providing farmers with the data-driven insights they need to optimize crop yields, improve resource efficiency, and adapt to the challenges posed by climate change. By leveraging machine learning technologies, farmers can make more informed decisions about everything from crop selection and planting schedules to pest management and market access. The benefits of these innovations extend beyond individual farmers, with implications for food security, economic development, and poverty reduction across the continent. As machine learning continues to evolve, its role in shaping the future of African agriculture will only grow, offering new opportunities for farmers, rural communities, and the continent as a whole to thrive in a rapidly changing world.

7

Machine Learning in Healthcare: Tackling Africa's Health Challenges

The healthcare sector in Africa faces an array of challenges that range from limited access to quality medical care to a shortage of healthcare professionals, and from the ongoing burden of infectious diseases to the growing threat of non-communicable diseases. These issues are compounded by underdeveloped infrastructure, unequal distribution of healthcare resources, and the high cost of medical treatments, particularly in rural and underserved areas. Machine learning, however, offers the potential to address many of these challenges by providing new tools for diagnosis, disease prevention, and resource optimization that can improve patient outcomes while reducing costs.

One of the most promising applications of machine learning in African healthcare is disease diagnosis. Machine learning algorithms can analyze medical images, such as X-rays, MRIs, and CT scans, to identify signs of diseases like tuberculosis, pneumonia, and cancer. This is particularly valuable in regions where healthcare professionals are in short supply and access to diagnostic equipment is limited. For instance, in many rural clinics, patients may not have access to a radiologist or specialist who can accurately interpret medical images. Machine learning algorithms trained on thousands of medical images can provide an accurate diagnosis within seconds, enabling healthcare workers to make more informed decisions about patient care. By improving the speed and accuracy of diagnosis, machine learning can help reduce the burden on overworked healthcare professionals and ensure that patients receive timely and effective treatments.

In addition to improving diagnosis, machine learning is also being used to analyze patient data and predict health outcomes. By examining electronic health records, lab results, and other clinical data, machine learning models can predict the likelihood of a patient developing certain conditions, such as diabetes, hypertension, or cardiovascular disease. These predictive models enable healthcare providers to identify high-risk patients early and intervene before the condition worsens. Preventive care is especially important in Africa, where healthcare systems are often stretched thin, and resources are limited. By allowing healthcare providers to focus on patients who are most at risk, machine learning can help optimize resource allocation, reduce hospital admissions, and improve overall patient outcomes.

Public health is another area where machine learning can play a transformative role, particularly in disease surveillance and outbreak prediction. Africa has experienced numerous outbreaks of infectious diseases, including Ebola, malaria, and cholera, which can spread rapidly and overwhelm healthcare systems. Machine learning models can analyze data on disease transmission, population movement, weather patterns, and other environmental factors to predict where and when an outbreak is likely to occur. For example, during an Ebola outbreak, machine learning algorithms can help identify high-risk areas based on data about human mobility, rainfall, and other variables. This enables public health authorities to deploy medical personnel, supplies, and interventions to the affected areas before the outbreak reaches a critical stage. By providing early warnings and enabling more targeted responses, machine learning can help reduce the spread of infectious diseases and save lives.

Beyond infectious diseases, machine learning is also being used to address chronic diseases, which are becoming increasingly prevalent in Africa. Non-communicable diseases (NCDs) such as diabetes, hypertension, and cancer are rising sharply, partly due to lifestyle changes, urbanization, and increased life expectancy. Managing these conditions requires long-term monitoring, early detection, and personalized treatment plans, all of which can be enhanced through machine learning. For example, machine learning algorithms can analyze patient data to predict when a diabetic patient is at risk of developing complications, such as kidney failure or heart disease, allowing healthcare providers to intervene early. Similarly, machine learning models can recommend personalized treatment plans based on a patient's medical history, genetic makeup, and lifestyle factors, ensuring that treatments are tailored to the individual's needs.

Telemedicine, powered by machine learning, is also playing a crucial role in expanding access to healthcare in Africa. In many rural and remote areas, access to doctors and medical facilities is limited, forcing patients to travel long distances for treatment. Telemedicine platforms enable patients to consult with healthcare providers via video calls or messaging apps, reducing the need for physical visits to clinics or hospitals. Machine learning algorithms can analyze a patient's symptoms, medical history, and other data to provide preliminary diagnoses and recommend treatment options. For instance, if a patient presents with symptoms of malaria or a respiratory infection, a machine learning-powered telemedicine system can quickly analyze the symptoms and recommend the appropriate medication or suggest further tests. This allows healthcare providers to focus on the most urgent cases while providing remote care for less severe conditions, improving the efficiency of healthcare delivery.

Drug discovery and personalized medicine are other areas where machine learning is making significant strides in healthcare. Traditional drug development is a time-consuming and expensive process, but machine learning can accelerate this process by analyzing vast datasets to identify potential drug candidates more quickly. In Africa, where certain diseases, such as sickle cell anemia and malaria, are more prevalent, machine learning can help researchers identify new treatments tailored to the specific genetic and environmental factors that affect African populations. Personalized medicine, which involves customizing treatment plans based on a patient's unique genetic makeup, medical history, and lifestyle, is also becoming more feasible thanks to machine learning. By analyzing patient data, machine learning models can recommend treatments that are more likely to be effective, reducing the trial-and-error approach that often characterizes traditional medical treatments.

Despite the many potential benefits of machine learning in African healthcare, there are several challenges that must be addressed to ensure its successful implementation. One of the most significant challenges is the lack of digital infrastructure, particularly in rural areas where internet connectivity is limited, and access to electronic health records (EHR) is rare. Without reliable digital systems for storing and sharing medical data, it can be difficult to integrate machine learning into healthcare practices. Investments in digital infrastructure are essential to ensure that machine learning technologies can be deployed effectively and reach the areas where they are needed most.

Data privacy and security are also critical concerns, particularly as healthcare data becomes more digitized and shared across platforms.

Machine learning algorithms require access to large amounts of data to be effective, but this raises questions about how sensitive patient information is protected. Ensuring that data is anonymized and used responsibly is essential to building trust in machine learning-powered healthcare solutions. Governments and healthcare providers must implement robust data protection regulations to safeguard patient privacy and ensure that data is not misused.

Another challenge is the shortage of healthcare professionals with the skills and knowledge to implement and manage machine learning technologies. While machine learning can augment the work of doctors, nurses, and healthcare workers, it requires trained professionals who can interpret the results generated by machine learning algorithms and apply them to clinical practice. Capacity-building programs and training initiatives are needed to equip healthcare professionals with the necessary skills to effectively use machine learning tools in their work.

In conclusion, machine learning has the potential to revolutionize healthcare in Africa by improving disease diagnosis, predicting health outcomes, optimizing resource allocation, and advancing personalized medicine. By providing healthcare providers with new tools for analyzing patient data, machine learning can help address many of the challenges that Africa's healthcare systems face, from limited access to medical professionals to the growing burden of chronic diseases. As machine learning technologies continue to evolve, their role in shaping the future of healthcare in Africa will only grow, offering new opportunities to improve patient outcomes, reducing costs, and making healthcare more accessible and equitable across the continent.

8

Education and Skill Development for Machine Learning in Africa

For machine learning to reach its full potential in Africa, the development of a skilled workforce that can develop, deploy, and managing machine learning technologies is essential. While Africa has a growing pool of tech talent, there remains a significant gap in expertise when it comes to machine learning, artificial intelligence (AI), and data science. Bridging this skills gap is crucial for ensuring that African countries can fully leverage the opportunities that machine learning presents across industries such as healthcare, agriculture, finance, and education. Governments, educational institutions, private companies, and international organizations all have a role to play in cultivating the skills and knowledge needed to drive machine learning innovation across the continent.

One of the biggest challenges in building machine learning capacity in Africa is the limited availability of formal education and training programs focused on AI and data science. While some universities across the continent are beginning to offer specialized programs in these fields, they remain relatively rare, and the resources needed to expand such programs are often in short supply. Many students who are interested in pursuing careers in machine learning may not have access to advanced courses or the necessary infrastructure, such as powerful computing resources, to fully explore the field. In addition, African universities often face challenges such as outdated curricula, limited funding for research, and a shortage of qualified instructors with expertise in machine learning and AI.

Addressing these challenges requires targeted investments in education and infrastructure. Governments and private institutions must prioritize the development of academic programs that focus on machine learning, AI, and data science, ensuring that students across the continent have access to world-class education in these fields. This may involve revising curricula to reflect the latest advancements in technology, providing scholarships to encourage students to pursue careers in data science, and investing in research facilities that can support cutting-edge work in machine learning. Partnerships between universities, governments, and the private sector will be essential in creating programs that not only train students but also equip them with the practical skills needed to address local challenges through machine learning.

In recent years, several initiatives have emerged to address the machine learning skills gap in Africa. One such initiative is the "Data Science Africa" program, which hosts workshops, conferences, and training programs aimed at building capacity in machine learning and data science across the continent. These events bring together academics, researchers, and industry professionals to share knowledge and collaborate on projects that address local issues, such as healthcare, agriculture, and urban planning. By providing hands-on training and access to cutting-edge tools and technologies, Data Science Africa helps build a community of practitioners who are equipped to apply machine learning solutions to the unique challenges faced by African countries.

Another key initiative is the "African Institute for Mathematical Sciences" (AIMS), which offers specialized programs in fields such as data science, machine learning, and artificial intelligence. AIMS to train the next generation of African scientists and innovators by providing students with access to top-tier education and research opportunities. By collaborating with industry partners, AIMS ensures that its graduates are equipped with the skills and knowledge needed to drive machine learning innovation in a wide range of sectors. AIMS also plays an important role in promoting collaboration between academia and industry, helping bridge the gap between theoretical knowledge and practical application in real-world settings.

In addition to formal educational programs, online platforms are becoming an increasingly important resource for building machine learning skills in Africa. Massive Open Online Courses (MOOCs) offered by platforms such as Coursera, edX, and Udemy provide African students with access to high-quality machine learning courses taught by experts from leading universities and tech companies. These platforms offer flexible learning opportunities, allowing students to study at their own pace while gaining practical skills that can be immediately applied in the workforce. By making machine learning education more accessible, online platforms help democratize access to knowledge and create a more inclusive tech ecosystem across Africa.

Private sector organizations also play a critical role in promoting machine learning education and skill development on the continent. Tech companies such as Google, Microsoft, and IBM have launched initiatives aimed at building AI and machine learning capacity in Africa. Google's "AI for Africa" program, for example, provides training, mentorship, and resources to African developers, researchers, and startups working in the AI space. The program focuses on equipping individuals and organizations with the tools they need to apply AI to local challenges, whether in healthcare, agriculture, or education. Similarly, Microsoft's "AI for Good" initiative seeks to leverage AI and machine learning to tackle pressing social and environmental challenges in Africa, while IBM's "Data Science Elite" team provides pro bono support to African companies and organizations looking to implement AI and machine learning solutions.

While these initiatives are helping to build machine learning capacity across Africa, much more needs to be done to ensure that the continent can fully capitalize on the opportunities that AI and machine learning present. One of the key challenges is ensuring that machine learning education and training programs are inclusive and accessible to all, regardless of socioeconomic background or geographic location. In many rural areas, access to the internet and digital devices remains limited, making it difficult for students to participate in online learning programs or take advantage of resources such as MOOCs. Governments and private companies will need to invest in expanding internet connectivity, improving access to digital tools, and building infrastructure that supports digital learning, particularly in underserved communities.

Another challenge is ensuring that machine learning education is tailored to the specific needs and contexts of African countries. Much of the existing machine learning curriculum is designed for students in more developed countries, and it may not fully address the unique challenges faced by African students and professionals. For example, there is a growing need for localized machine learning applications in areas such as agriculture, healthcare, and urban development, yet many training programs still focus on generic use cases that are not necessarily relevant to African contexts. Developing localized curricula that emphasize the practical application of machine learning to African challenges will be crucial in ensuring that the next generation of African machine learning experts is well-prepared to address the continent's most pressing issues.

The importance of collaboration between academia, industry, and government cannot be overstated. By working together, these stakeholders can create a robust ecosystem that supports the growth of machine learning talent across Africa. Governments can provide funding and policy support to educational institutions, while private companies can offer mentorship, internships, and job opportunities to students and graduates. Academia, in turn, can play a leading role in research and innovation, developing new machine learning models and algorithms that address Africa-specific challenges. International organizations can also contribute by providing technical expertise, funding, and resources to support machine learning education and skill development initiatives across the continent.

In conclusion, the development of machine learning skills is critical to Africa's future in the global digital economy. As machine learning continues to transform industries and drive innovation around the world, it is essential that Africa builds a strong foundation of talent capable of harnessing the power of AI to solve local challenges. While there are significant barriers to overcome, including a lack of formal education programs and digital infrastructure, initiatives such as Data Science Africa, AIMS, and online learning platforms are helping to build the skills needed to drive machine learning innovation across the continent. By investing in education, infrastructure, and collaboration, African countries can ensure that their tech ecosystems are well-equipped to take full advantage of the opportunities that machine learning offers, paving the way for a more prosperous and technologically advanced future.

9

Smart Cities in Africa: Leveraging Machine Learning for Urbanization

As Africa continues to experience rapid urbanization, the demand for sustainable and efficient city infrastructure is becoming increasingly urgent. African cities are among the fastest-growing in the world, with urban populations expected to triple by 2050. While urbanization brings opportunities for economic growth, innovation, and cultural development, it also presents significant challenges, including inadequate infrastructure, traffic congestion, waste management, housing shortages, and uneven access to essential services. Machine learning offers a suite of powerful tools that can help African cities address these challenges and become smarter, more sustainable, and better equipped to meet the needs of their growing populations.

Urban planning is one of the most critical areas where machine learning can make a significant impact. Traditionally, urban planning has been a slow, manual process, often based on outdated data and limited resources. As African cities grow, planners must decide where to build new infrastructure, such as roads, schools, hospitals, and housing, while ensuring that these developments are aligned with the needs of the population. Machine learning can assist in this process by analyzing large datasets from sources like satellite imagery, population growth trends, transportation patterns, and resource usage statistics. By providing real-time insights into how cities are evolving, machine learning models can help urban planners make more informed decisions that lead to the creation of well-organized, efficient urban spaces that accommodate rapid population growth while minimizing environmental impact.

For example, in cities like Lagos and Nairobi, where traffic congestion has become a significant problem, machine learning algorithms can be used to optimize traffic management systems. Traffic congestion results in lost productivity, increased pollution, and reduced quality of life for residents. Machine learning models can analyze data from GPS devices, traffic cameras, mobile apps, and public transport systems to predict traffic patterns, adjust traffic light timings, and recommend alternative routes to drivers. These algorithms can also help city planners redesign roads, implement carpooling incentives, and develop smart public transportation networks that alleviate the burden on the roads.

Public transportation stands to benefit from the integration of machine learning. Many African cities rely on informal transport systems such as minibuses, motorcycle taxis, and shared rides, which are often poorly regulated and difficult to manage. Machine learning models can analyze data on public transportation usage to optimize routes, predict demand, and allocate resources more efficiently. For example, algorithms can identify peak hours and busiest routes, allowing transport providers to increase vehicle availability in high-demand areas. By improving the efficiency and reliability of public transportation systems, machine learning can encourage more people to use these services, reducing reliance on private vehicles and alleviating traffic congestion.

Energy management is another area where machine learning can contribute to the development of smarter cities. Many African cities face frequent power outages, energy shortages, and unreliable access to electricity, which can hamper economic growth and reduce quality of life. Machine learning can help optimize energy consumption and distribution by analyzing data from smart meters, energy grids, and weather forecasts. For example, algorithms can predict periods of peak energy demand and recommend strategies to balance the load, such as encouraging consumers to shift energy use to off-peak hours. In addition, machine learning models can optimize the integration of renewable energy sources, such as solar and wind, into the grid. These models can predict the amount of energy that will be generated by renewable sources based on weather patterns, allowing energy providers to plan accordingly and reduce reliance on fossil fuels.

In addition to optimizing energy distribution, machine learning can also improve the efficiency of water and waste management systems in African cities. Many cities struggle with inadequate waste disposal systems, leading to pollution, health hazards, and environmental degradation. Machine learning models can help city governments and waste management companies optimize waste collection routes, predict when waste bins will be full, and ensure that waste is processed and recycled in the most efficient manner. In Cape Town, South Africa, for instance, machine learning has been used to optimize water management during periods of drought by predicting water usage patterns and recommending ways to conserve water resources. By improving the efficiency of water and waste management systems, machine learning can contribute to the creation of cleaner, more sustainable urban environments.

Public safety is another critical aspect of smart city development where machine learning can play an important role. Crime rates in many African cities, particularly in informal settlements and high-density areas, pose significant challenges to urban safety. Machine learning algorithms can analyze data from surveillance cameras, social media feeds, and police reports to predict crime hotspots and recommend preventive measures. For example, predictive policing models can identify patterns in criminal activity and suggest where law enforcement resources should be deployed to prevent incidents. While predictive policing has raised concerns about potential biases in data and privacy issues, when implemented responsibly, it has the potential to improve public safety and reduce crime rates in urban areas.

In addition to helping cities manage infrastructure and public safety, machine learning can also improve the delivery of essential services such as healthcare and education. In many African cities, access to healthcare facilities and educational institutions is unevenly distributed, with underserved communities often facing significant barriers to accessing these services. Machine learning models can be used to analyze demographic and geographic data to identify gaps in service provision and recommend strategies for allocating resources more equitably. For example, algorithms can predict where new schools or hospitals should be built based on population growth patterns, transportation access, and the proximity of existing facilities. This can help ensure that all urban residents have access to the services they need, regardless of their socioeconomic status or location within the city.

Despite the many potential benefits of machine learning for smart city development in Africa, there are several challenges that must be addressed to ensure successful implementation. One of the primary challenges is the lack of digital infrastructure in many African cities, particularly in informal settlements and underserved areas. Reliable internet connectivity, access to data, and the ability to collect and process information in real-time are essential for deploying machine learning solutions effectively. Governments and private sector organizations will need to invest in building the necessary infrastructure to support machine learning applications in urban environments. This may involve expanding broadband access, implementing citywide sensor networks, and ensuring that urban planners and city officials have the tools they need to make data-driven decisions.

Another challenge is ensuring that smart city initiatives are inclusive and equitable. As cities adopt machine learning and other digital technologies, there is a risk that marginalized communities could be left behind, particularly if they lack access to the internet, digital devices, or the skills needed to participate in the digital economy. Smart city solutions must be designed with inclusive in mind, ensuring that all residents, regardless of their socioeconomic status, benefit from the improvements in infrastructure, transportation, and services that these technologies offer. Collaboration between governments, civil society organizations, and the private sector will be essential to ensure that smart city initiatives are implemented in a way that promotes social equity and reduces urban inequality.

In conclusion, machine learning has the potential to transform African cities by optimizing urban planning, transportation, energy management, waste disposal, public safety, and the delivery of essential services. By leveraging data-driven insights, African cities can become more efficient, sustainable, and resilient in the face of rapid urbanization. However, realizing the full potential of machine learning in urban environments will require significant investments in digital infrastructure, as well as a commitment to ensuring that smart city initiatives are inclusive and accessible to all residents. As African cities continue to grow, machine learning will play an increasingly important role in shaping their future, helping to build cities that are not only smarter but also more sustainable and equitable for all.

10

Machine Learning and Renewable Energy in Africa

Energy is a crucial driver of economic development, and yet millions of people across Africa still lack access to reliable and affordable electricity. As African countries strive to meet their growing energy needs, they are also facing the challenge of transitioning to more sustainable energy sources. Renewable energy, particularly solar, wind, and hydropower, has the potential to transform Africa's energy landscape by providing clean, affordable, and reliable power. However, integrating renewable energy into the grid and managing energy demand effectively is a complex task, especially given the variability of renewable energy sources. This is where machine learning can play a pivotal role.

Machine learning offers powerful tools for optimizing energy production, distribution, and consumption. By analyzing vast amounts of data on weather patterns, energy usage, and grid performance, machine learning algorithms can help energy providers make better decisions about when and where to generate, store, and distribute electricity. This can lead to more efficient use of renewable energy resources, reduced energy costs, and increased access to electricity for underserved communities.

One of the key challenges in managing energy systems is predicting demand. Energy consumption patterns can fluctuate significantly depending on factors such as time of day, weather conditions, and economic activity. Traditional methods of predicting energy demand are often based on historical data, which may not always reflect real-time changes in consumption patterns. Machine learning models, on the other hand, can analyze large datasets in real-time to make more accurate predictions about future energy demand. These models can take into account a wide range of variables, such as weather forecasts, population movements, and economic activity, to predict when and where energy demand will be highest. This allows energy providers to better manage supply and avoid power outages, which are common in many parts of Africa.

In addition to predicting demand, machine learning can also help optimize the integration of renewable energy sources into the grid. Renewable energy, particularly solar and wind, is inherently variable, as it depends on factors such as sunlight and wind speed, which can change from hour to hour or day to day. This variability makes it challenging to ensure a stable supply of electricity from renewable sources. Machine learning models can analyze data from weather forecasts, satellite imagery, and historical energy production patterns to predict how much energy will be generated by renewable sources at any given time. By providing accurate forecasts of renewable energy production, machine learning can help energy providers plan more effectively and ensure that the grid remains stable even when renewable energy generation fluctuates.

Energy storage is another critical area where machine learning can make a significant impact. One of the challenges of renewable energy is that it is often generated when demand is low, leading to surplus energy that must be stored for later use. For example, solar energy is typically produced during the day, when demand for electricity may be lower, but it is needed most in the evening when people return home from work. Machine learning algorithms can optimize the operation of energy storage systems, such as batteries, by predicting when energy will be needed and ensuring that stored energy is released at the right time. This can help reduce reliance on fossil fuels and ensure that renewable energy is available when it is needed most.

Machine learning can also improve the efficiency of energy distribution. In many African countries, energy losses during transmission and distribution are a significant problem, leading to higher costs for consumers and reduced reliability of electricity supply. Machine learning models can analyze data from power grids to detect inefficiencies and recommend strategies for improving energy distribution. For example, algorithms can optimize the routing of electricity through the grid to minimize losses and ensure that energy is delivered to where it is needed most. By improving the efficiency of energy distribution, machine learning can help reduce energy costs and increase access to electricity for underserved communities.

In rural areas, where access to the grid may be limited or nonexistent, machine learning can support the development of decentralized energy systems, such as microgrids. Microgrids are small-scale energy systems that can operate independently of the main grid, providing power to communities that are not connected to the national grid. These systems are often powered by renewable energy sources, such as solar panels or wind turbines, and are particularly valuable in remote or rural areas where extending the national grid may be cost-prohibitive. Machine learning models can optimize the operation of microgrids by predicting energy demand, managing energy storage, and integrating renewable energy sources. By making decentralized energy systems more efficient, machine learning can help bring electricity to underserved communities and support rural development.

In addition to optimizing energy production and distribution, machine learning can also play a role in energy conservation. Many African countries are working to reduce their reliance on fossil fuels and transition to more sustainable energy sources. However, energy conservation is essential to ensuring that renewable energy resources are used efficiently, and that energy demand does not outstrip supply. Machine learning models can analyze data on energy usage patterns to identify opportunities for reducing energy consumption. For example, alternative methods can recommend energy-saving strategies for households and businesses, such as adjusting thermostat settings, using energy-efficient appliances, or shifting energy-intensive activities to off-peak hours when electricity demand is lower. By helping consumers and businesses reduce their energy consumption, machine learning can support the transition to a more sustainable energy system.

Despite the many benefits that machine learning offers for the renewable energy sector, there are challenges that must be addressed to ensure its successful implementation in Africa. One of the key challenges is the lack of reliable data on energy production and consumption, particularly in rural areas. Without accurate data, machine learning models may struggle to provide accurate predictions and recommendations. In many parts of Africa, energy data is still collected manually, and there is limited infrastructure for real-time monitoring of energy systems. Investments in digital infrastructure, such as smart meters and sensors, are essential to support the collection and analysis of energy data.

Another challenge is the need for skilled professionals who can develop and manage machine learning models for the energy sector. While Africa has a growing pool of tech talent, there is still a shortage of professionals with expertise in machine learning and energy systems. Training programs and capacity-building initiatives will be critical to ensuring that African countries can develop the local expertise needed to implement machine learning solutions for renewable energy. Governments, universities, and private companies must work together to create educational programs that equip students and professionals with the skills they need to drive innovation in the energy sector.

Collaboration between governments, energy providers, and tech companies will also be essential to ensuring the successful deployment of machine learning technologies in the energy sector. Governments can play a key role by creating policies that support the adoption of renewable energy and the use of machine learning for energy management. Energy providers can invest in machine learning technologies to improve the efficiency of their operations and reduce costs, while tech companies can develop the algorithms and tools needed to analyze energy data and optimize energy systems. By working together, these stakeholders can accelerate the transition to a more sustainable and resilient energy system in Africa.

In conclusion, machine learning has the potential to play a transformative role in Africa's energy transition by optimizing energy production, integrating renewable energy sources, improving energy storage, and supporting decentralized energy systems. By leveraging the power of machine learning, African countries can build more sustainable, reliable, and affordable energy systems that meet the needs of their growing populations. While there are challenges to overcome, including the need for reliable data and skilled professionals, the opportunities for machine learning in the renewable energy sector are vast. As Africa continues to embrace renewable energy, machine learning will be a critical tool for ensuring that the continent's energy future is both sustainable and inclusive.

11

Machine Learning for Environmental Sustainability in Africa

Environmental sustainability is a pressing issue in Africa, where the continent's rich natural resources and diverse ecosystems face increasing threats from deforestation, desertification, water scarcity, and climate change. Africa is experiencing rapid economic development and urbanization, which places additional stress on its environment. Balancing economic growth with environmental protection is essential to ensuring a sustainable future for Africa. Machine learning presents a range of tools that can help address these challenges by providing data-driven insights to monitor natural resources, reduce environmental impact, and promote sustainability across key sectors such as agriculture, energy, and waste management.

One of the most important applications of machine learning in promoting environmental sustainability is in monitoring and managing natural resources. Africa's forests, water sources, and biodiversity are under continuous pressure from human activity, climate change, and resource extraction. Machine learning can be used to analyze satellite imagery and remote sensing data to monitor environmental changes in real-time. For example, machine learning algorithms can track deforestation by identifying patterns of illegal logging, land-use change, and forest degradation. With the help of these insights, governments and conservation organizations can take preventive action to protect forests and combat illegal activities before significant damage is done.

In addition to deforestation, machine learning models can help monitor wildlife populations and habitats, which are critical for biodiversity conservation. By analyzing data on animal movements, habitat conditions, and threats such as poaching, machine learning can provide insights into wildlife population health and predict where conservation efforts should be focused. In regions where endangered species such as elephants, rhinos, and gorillas are at risk from poaching, machine learning algorithms can be used to identify poaching hotspots and guide law enforcement efforts. The ability to track wildlife and monitor habitats in real-time can improve the effectiveness of conservation programs and help protect Africa's unique biodiversity.

Water management is another area where machine learning can play a crucial role in ensuring environmental sustainability. Water scarcity is a growing concern across many African regions, particularly in arid and semi-arid areas where agricultural productivity is heavily dependent on irrigation. Machine learning models can analyze weather patterns, soil moisture levels, and water consumption data to predict water availability and recommend more efficient water usage strategies. For instance, farmers can use machine learning-powered irrigation systems that automatically adjust water application based on real-time data, ensuring that crops receive the right amount of water without overuse or wastage. This technology helps farmers conserve water, improve crop yields, and reduce the environmental impact of agriculture, which is one of the largest consumers of freshwater in Africa.

Beyond water management, machine learning is also playing a role in supporting the continent's transition to renewable energy. Africa has vast potential for renewable energy generation, particularly from solar and wind power, but the challenge lies in efficiently integrating these energy sources into the power grid. Machine learning can optimize renewable energy production by analyzing data on weather patterns, energy demand, and grid performance. For instance, machine learning algorithms can predict periods of high solar or wind energy generation and ensure that the grid can accommodate these fluctuations. This leads to a more stable energy supply and reduces reliance on fossil fuels, which contribute to carbon emissions and environmental degradation. Machine learning also helps energy companies plan for energy storage, ensuring that renewable energy is available even during periods of low generation.

Sustainable farming practices are another important area where machine learning is having a significant impact. Agriculture is a major source of both livelihoods and environmental degradation in Africa. Conventional farming methods often lead to soil erosion, deforestation, and overuse of chemical inputs, which harm ecosystems and reduce long-term agricultural productivity. Machine learning provides farmers with the ability to adopt more sustainable practices by analyzing data on soil health, crop performance, and environmental conditions. By offering recommendations on the optimal use of fertilizers and pesticides, machine learning can reduce the environmental impact of farming and promote agroecological practices such as crop rotation and intercropping, which enhance soil fertility and biodiversity. Sustainable farming practices not only benefit the environment but also improve the resilience of agricultural systems to the impacts of climate change, such as droughts and floods.

Waste management is another critical area where machine learning can support environmental sustainability in Africa. As urban populations grow, waste generation is increasing, and many African cities struggle to manage the mounting volumes of solid waste. Poor waste management can lead to environmental pollution, public health risks, and the contamination of water sources. Machine learning can help cities optimize waste collection and recycling processes by analyzing data on waste generation patterns, landfill capacity, and recycling rates. For example, machine learning algorithms can predict when waste bins will be full and recommend the most efficient collection routes for waste disposal trucks. This helps cities reduce operational costs, improve recycling rates, and minimize the environmental impact of waste.

Machine learning can also contribute to environmental sustainability by informing environmental policy and decision-making. Policymakers face complex trade-offs between economic development and environmental protection, and machine learning models can help them better understand the potential impacts of their decisions. By analyzing data on land use, economic activity, and resource consumption, machine learning can provide insights into how different policy choices will affect the environment. This can lead to more informed decisions about infrastructure development, resource allocation, and environmental regulations, ensuring that economic growth does not come at the expense of Africa's natural resources.

Despite the promise of machine learning for environmental sustainability, several challenges must be addressed to ensure its successful implementation in Africa. One of the most significant challenges is the availability of reliable environmental data. In many parts of Africa, data on air and water quality, deforestation, and biodiversity is either scarce or difficult to access. Without accurate data, machine learning models may struggle to provide actionable insights. Addressing this challenge will require investment in environmental monitoring infrastructure, such as sensors, satellite networks, and data-sharing platforms that allow stakeholders to collect and analyze environmental data more effectively.

Another challenge is ensuring that machine learning solutions are accessible to local communities, decision-makers, and environmental organizations. Machine learning models can produce valuable insights, but these insights must be communicated in ways that are easy to understand and apply. This will require collaboration between technologists, environmental scientists, and community leaders to ensure that machine learning tools are tailored to the specific needs and contexts of different regions in Africa. By building partnerships and ensuring that machine learning solutions are locally relevant, African countries can maximize the potential of this technology to support environmental sustainability.

In conclusion, machine learning has the potential to play a transformative role in promoting environmental sustainability across Africa. From monitoring natural resources and wildlife conservation to optimizing water and energy use, machine learning provides new tools for addressing the continent's most pressing environmental challenges. As Africa continues to develop, ensuring that machine learning is used in ways that protect the environment and promote sustainability will be critical to securing a sustainable future for the continent. While challenges such as data availability and accessibility remain, the benefits of applying machine learning to environmental management are clear, and the technology will play an increasingly important role in supporting Africa's transition to a greener, more sustainable future.

12

Policy and Regulation for Machine Learning in African Markets

The widespread adoption of machine learning across African markets presents both incredible opportunities and unique challenges. While the potential for machine learning to transform industries such as healthcare, finance, agriculture, and energy is immense, ensuring the responsible and ethical deployment of this technology requires robust policy and regulatory frameworks. As machine learning continues to evolve and become more deeply integrated into various sectors, African governments must establish clear regulations to address issues such as data privacy, transparency, algorithmic fairness, and the broader social impacts of automation. The development of effective policy and regulatory frameworks will be crucial to promoting innovation while safeguarding public interests and ensuring that machine learning benefits all segments of society.

One of the most urgent regulatory issues surrounding machine learning in Africa is data privacy. Machine learning algorithms depend on large datasets to make predictions and optimize processes, but these datasets often include sensitive personal information, such as financial transactions, medical records, or location data. In Africa, where data privacy regulations are still in the early stages of development, there is a critical need for clear guidelines governing how data is collected, stored, and used by organizations deploying machine learning technologies. Some African countries, such as South Africa with the Protection of Personal Information Act (POPIA), Nigeria with the Nigeria Data Protection Regulation (NDPR), and Kenya with the Data Protection Act (DPA), have taken steps toward creating data privacy frameworks. However, many African countries lack comprehensive data protection laws, and even where regulations exist, enforcement can be inconsistent.

Ensuring that data privacy regulations keep pace with technological advancements is essential. Machine learning-driven industries, such as fintech, healthcare, and telecommunications, rely heavily on personal data, and the potential for misuse or unauthorized access to sensitive information is high. To address these concerns, African governments must develop and enforce strong data protection laws that prioritize individual privacy and ensure that personal data is handled responsibly. Regulators should also establish clear standards for how data is anonymized to prevent unauthorized identification of individuals. Data protection authorities need to work closely with industry players to ensure that privacy protocols are built into machine learning systems from the outset, allowing for the responsible and secure use of personal data.

In addition to data privacy, algorithmic transparency is another major concern that policymakers must address. Machine learning models are often described as "black boxes" because they operate in ways that are not easily understood by humans. These models can make critical decisions—such as whether a person qualifies for a loan, receives healthcare treatment, or is hired for a job—without clear explanations of how those decisions are reached. The lack of transparency in machine learning algorithms can lead to discrimination, bias, and unfair outcomes. For example, if a model is trained on biased data, it may produce biased results, disproportionately affecting certain groups based on race, gender, or socioeconomic status.

To ensure fairness and accountability in machine learning systems, African regulators should require greater transparency from companies that use these technologies. This can involve mandating that organizations provide clear explanations of how their machine learning models work and how decisions are made. For high-stakes applications such as credit scoring, medical diagnoses, or hiring, organizations should be required to demonstrate that their models are free from bias and comply with ethical guidelines. Regulators can also encourage the development of explainable AI, a branch of artificial intelligence focused on making machine learning models more interpretable. By promoting transparency, African governments can help build public trust in machine learning technologies and ensure that they are used in ways that benefit society.

Algorithmic fairness and bias are particularly important issues in African markets, where social and economic inequalities are prevalent. Machine learning models that perpetuate biases can exacerbate existing inequalities and create new forms of discrimination. For example, in the financial sector, biased machine learning algorithms could deny credit to individuals from marginalized communities, reinforcing economic disparities. Similarly, biased healthcare algorithms could result in substandard care for certain groups, further entrenching healthcare inequalities. To address these risks, African policymakers must develop guidelines that ensure machine learning systems are tested for fairness and do not perpetuate harmful biases. This may involve creating regulatory bodies or oversight committees tasked with evaluating the fairness of machine learning models and ensuring that they comply with anti-discrimination laws.

Another major concern surrounding the adoption of machine learning in African markets is its impact on employment and the future of work. While machine learning has the potential to increase productivity and create new economic opportunities, it also has the potential to displace workers, particularly in industries that rely on manual labor or repetitive tasks. Automation, powered by machine learning, is likely to affect sectors such as agriculture, manufacturing, logistics, and retail, where jobs may be replaced by intelligent machines or algorithms. In a continent where unemployment and underemployment are already significant challenges, policymakers must consider how to mitigate the potential social impact of automation.

One approach to addressing the displacement of workers by machine learning is to invest in education and workforce development programs. African governments, educational institutions, and private sector organizations must work together to equip workers with the skills needed for the jobs of the future. This includes providing training in areas such as data science, machine learning, AI development, and other digital skills that are in high demand in the global economy. By focusing on reskilling and upskilling programs, African countries can help workers transition to new roles in the digital economy, ensuring that they remain competitive in an increasingly automated world. Additionally, policymakers can explore policies such as universal basic income (UBI) or social safety nets to support workers whose jobs may be displaced by automation.

The financial sector is one of the areas where machine learning presents both significant opportunities and regulatory challenges. On the one hand, machine learning can expand access to financial services by enabling alternative credit scoring mechanisms for individuals who lack traditional credit histories. This has the potential to promote financial inclusion and provide underserved populations with access to loans, insurance, and other financial products. However, the use of machine learning in financial services also raises concerns about consumer protection, algorithmic bias, and the potential for financial instability. Regulators must strike a balance between encouraging innovation and ensuring that financial institutions use machine learning responsibly.

In healthcare, machine learning offers the potential to revolutionize disease diagnosis, patient care, and medical research. However, the use of machine learning in clinical settings must be carefully regulated to ensure that patient safety is not compromised. For example, machine learning models used to diagnose diseases must be rigorously tested to ensure their accuracy and reliability. Regulators must also address issues such as data privacy, particularly as healthcare data becomes increasingly digitized and shared across platforms. Clear guidelines on the use of machine learning in healthcare will be essential to ensure that the technology improves patient outcomes without compromising ethical standards.

One of the key challenges in developing regulatory frameworks for machine learning in Africa is the need for cross-sector collaboration. Machine learning is being applied across a wide range of industries, from finance and healthcare to agriculture and energy, and each sector has its own unique regulatory requirements. African regulators must work together across sectors to develop comprehensive policies that address the specific challenges and opportunities of machine learning in each industry. This will require coordination between government agencies, industry stakeholders, and civil society organizations to ensure that machine learning is deployed in ways that promote innovation while protecting public interests.

Capacity building among regulators and policymakers is also critical to ensuring that African countries can develop effective regulatory frameworks for machine learning. Many regulators may lack the technical expertise needed to fully understand the implications of machine learning technologies, which are constantly evolving. Investing in education and training for regulators, as well as creating opportunities for collaboration with international organizations and AI experts, will be essential to building the capacity needed to regulate machine learning effectively.

In conclusion, policy and regulation will play a pivotal role in shaping the future of machine learning in African markets. By addressing issues such as data privacy, algorithmic transparency, fairness, and the societal impact of automation, African governments can ensure that machine learning is deployed in ways that benefit society and promote inclusive development. At the same time, policymakers must strike a balance between promoting innovation and ensuring that machine learning is used responsibly and ethically. As the technology continues to evolve, African countries will need to adapt their regulatory frameworks to meet the challenges and opportunities presented by machine learning, ensuring that it is a force for good across the continent.

13

Case Studies: Successful Machine Learning Applications in Africa

Machine learning has already begun to make a significant impact across various sectors in Africa, contributing to innovative solutions that address some of the continent's most pressing challenges. From agriculture and healthcare to finance and energy, African companies and organizations are leveraging machine learning to optimize processes, enhance decision-making, and improve service delivery. These efforts are not only driving economic growth but also improving the quality of life for millions of people across the continent. The following case studies highlight some of the most successful applications of machine learning in Africa, showcasing how technology is transforming industries and creating new opportunities for development.

Agriculture remains one of the most vital sectors for many African economies, but it is also one of the most challenging. Smallholder farmers, who make up a large portion of the continent's agricultural workforce, often lack access to the tools and resources they need to improve productivity and efficiency. One company addressing this issue is Hello Tractor, an agricultural technology firm based in Nigeria. Hello Tractor, has developed a platform that connects smallholder farmers with tractor owners, allowing farmers to rent tractors on demand. Machine learning is central to this platform, as it is used to analyze data on weather conditions, crop cycles, and tractor availability to ensure that tractors are deployed to farms at the most optimal times. Machine learning models help match farmers with tractor services in a way that maximizes efficiency and minimizes costs, leading to higher productivity for small-scale farmers. This solution has had a transformative effect on farming communities across Nigeria and other African countries by reducing the physical labor required for farming and increasing crop yields. Hello Tractor's, predictive maintenance feature, powered by machine learning, further enhances the platform's impact by analyzing real-time data from tractors to predict when maintenance is needed, thus reducing downtime and ensuring that tractors are available when farmers need them most.

In the healthcare sector, access to medical services is often limited, particularly in rural and underserved areas. Babyl Rwanda, a subsidiary of Babylon Health, is using machine learning to tackle this issue by providing AI-powered telemedicine services. Through Babyl Rwanda's platform, patients can consult with doctors remotely via their mobile phones, allowing them to receive medical advice without needing to travel long distances to a healthcare facility. Machine learning algorithms analyze the symptoms reported by patients and provide preliminary diagnoses and treatment recommendations, helping healthcare providers make more informed decisions. The platform also enables patients to schedule appointments with doctors for more in-depth consultations. By integrating machine learning into its system, Babyl Rwanda has improved access to healthcare for thousands of Rwandans, particularly those in remote areas where healthcare facilities are scarce. The platform also helps reduce the burden on healthcare workers by streamlining the diagnostic process and ensuring that patients receive timely care. This is particularly important in Africa, where healthcare systems are often overstretched and under-resourced.

Energy access is another critical issue in Africa, where millions of people live without reliable electricity. M-KOPA, a Kenyan-based company, is using machine learning to expand access to clean, affordable energy through its pay-as-you-go solar energy systems. M-KOPA's business model allows customers to purchase solar panels and home energy systems on credit, with payments made in small installments via mobile money platforms. Machine learning is used to assess the creditworthiness of customers by analyzing data on mobile phone usage, payment histories, and customer behavior. This approach enables M-KOPA to offer financing to individuals who may not have traditional credit histories, thus promoting financial inclusion. Additionally, machine learning helps optimize energy usage by predicting consumption patterns and ensuring that solar systems operate efficiently. This has helped M-KOPA bring solar energy to more than 750,000 households across East Africa, improving access to electricity for off-grid communities while reducing reliance on fossil fuels.

Financial inclusion is a significant challenge in Africa, where many people are excluded from the formal banking system due to a lack of credit history or access to financial institutions. Tala, a fintech company operating in Kenya, Tanzania, and Nigeria, is using machine learning to provide loans to underserved populations. Tala's mobile app allows users to apply for small loans directly from their smartphones. Instead of relying on traditional credit scores, Tala's machine learning models analyze alternative data sources, such as mobile phone usage, social media activity, and payment behavior, to assess an individual's creditworthiness. The algorithm provides an instant decision on whether a user qualifies for a loan, and funds are disbursed almost immediately if approved. Tala's use of machine learning has enabled it to provide loans to millions of people who would otherwise be unable to access credit, thereby promoting financial inclusion and supporting entrepreneurship. The platform's machine learning algorithms also continuously analyze repayment patterns, allowing Tala to offer personalized loan terms and adjust interest rates based on individual risk profiles. This approach not only helps Tala minimize default rates but also allows the company to build trust with its customers, many of whom are using formal financial services for the first time.

In the area of public safety, Zipline, a U.S.-based company with operations in Rwanda and Ghana, is using machine learning to power its drone delivery service for medical supplies. Zipline's drones deliver life-saving medical supplies such as blood, vaccines, and medications to remote and hard-to-reach areas where access to healthcare facilities is limited. Machine learning algorithms optimize the flight routes of Zipline's drones by analyzing data on weather conditions, terrain, and delivery urgency. These algorithms ensure that drones take the most efficient routes and avoid obstacles, thereby reducing delivery times and improving the reliability of the service. In addition to optimizing drone routes, Zipline uses machine learning to manage inventory levels at its distribution centers, predicting demand for medical supplies based on historical data and real-time trends. This helps ensure that critical medical supplies are available when needed, preventing shortages and improving healthcare outcomes in underserved regions. Zipline's innovative use of machine learning in logistics has saved countless lives by providing timely access to essential medical supplies in areas that would otherwise be difficult to reach.

Waste management is another area where machine learning is having a positive impact in Africa. As cities across the continent grow, managing the increasing volume of waste generated by urban populations has become a major challenge. Mr. Green Africa, a Kenyan company, is using machine learning to optimize its recycling operations and reduce the environmental impact of plastic waste. The company works with a network of informal waste collectors, purchasing recyclable materials from them and processing the materials into high-quality plastic that can be used by manufacturers. Machine learning is used to analyze data on waste generation patterns, recycling rates, and market demand, allowing Mr. Green Africa to optimize its collection and sorting processes. By predicting where and when recyclable materials will be generated, the company can deploy its waste collectors more efficiently, increasing the volume of plastic that is recovered and reducing the amount of waste that ends up in landfills. This approach not only helps address the growing waste management crisis in Kenya but also creates jobs for waste collectors, many of whom rely on this work as their primary source of income.

These case studies illustrate the diverse and transformative potential of machine learning in Africa. Whether it is improving agricultural productivity through smart farming, expanding access to healthcare with AI-powered telemedicine, promoting financial inclusion by using alternative credit scoring models, or optimizing waste management and energy consumption, machine learning is driving innovation and solving real-world problems across the continent. The success of these companies highlights the importance of using data-driven approaches to address the unique challenges facing African markets, and the potential for machine learning to create new opportunities for economic growth and social development. As the technology continues to evolve, the applications of machine learning in Africa will undoubtedly expand, offering even more possibilities for improving the lives of people across the continent.

14

The Future of Machine Learning in Africa

The future of machine learning in Africa is filled with immense potential as the continent continues to embrace technological innovation. With its diverse economies, youthful population, and increasing digital connectivity, Africa is uniquely positioned to harness the transformative power of machine learning to drive economic growth, enhance public services, and address societal challenges. As machine learning continues to evolve and its applications expand, Africa has the opportunity to become a leader in the global AI ecosystem, provided that the right investments are made in infrastructure, education, and policy frameworks.

One of the key drivers of the future of machine learning in Africa is the ongoing expansion of digital infrastructure. In recent years, there has been significant progress in increasing internet access and mobile phone penetration across the continent, but gaps remain, particularly in rural and underserved areas. Expanding access to high-speed internet and digital tools will be critical to unlocking the full potential of machine learning. As more Africans gain access to smartphones, cloud computing, and affordable data services, they will be able to participate in the digital economy and take advantage of machine learning applications in sectors such as agriculture, healthcare, education, and financial services. The growth of the Internet of Things (IoT) will also generate large amounts of data that can be used to train machine learning models, further driving innovation.

In parallel with the expansion of digital infrastructure, the rise of artificial intelligence (AI) research and development in Africa is expected to accelerate. Several African countries, including Kenya, South Africa, and Nigeria, are home to burgeoning AI research communities that are focused on developing solutions tailored to the continent's unique challenges. AI research centers and innovation hubs are being established across the continent, providing a platform for African researchers, entrepreneurs, and engineers to collaborate and develop machine learning solutions that address local needs. This growing ecosystem of AI innovation will be crucial in ensuring that Africa is not just a consumer of machine learning technologies but also a contributor to global advancements in the field.

Another important aspect of the future of machine learning in Africa is the need to cultivate a skilled workforce capable of developing and deploying machine learning systems. While there is no shortage of talent in Africa, there is a pressing need for more specialized education and training programs focused on data science, machine learning, and artificial intelligence. Universities, technical schools, and online learning platforms will play a central role in training the next generation of AI professionals. However, it will also be important to provide reskilling and upskilling opportunities for workers whose jobs may be impacted by automation. By investing in education and workforce development, African countries can ensure that their citizens are equipped with the skills needed to thrive in an AI-driven world and that they remain competitive in the global marketplace.

Machine learning also has the potential to promote more inclusive development across Africa, particularly by addressing the needs of marginalized and underserved communities. One of the most exciting aspects of machine learning is its ability to provide solutions that are scalable and accessible to populations in remote and rural areas. For example, AI-powered telemedicine platforms can connect patients with doctors in real-time, providing much-needed healthcare services to individuals in areas where medical facilities are scarce. Similarly, mobile money platforms powered by machine learning can offer financial services to individuals who were previously excluded from the formal banking system. As machine learning continues to evolve, its applications will become even more diverse, offering new ways to bridge the gap between urban and rural areas and ensure that underserved populations have access to essential services.

While the future of machine learning in Africa is full of promise, there are also challenges that must be addressed to ensure that the technology is deployed in ways that are ethical, fair, and beneficial to all. One of the key concerns is the risk of bias and discrimination in machine learning models. If these models are trained on biased datasets, they may produce outcomes that disproportionately disadvantage certain groups, such as women, ethnic minorities, or individuals from lower socioeconomic backgrounds. For example, biased algorithms could deny access to loans or employment opportunities based on characteristics that have no bearing on an individual's ability to repay a loan or perform a job. Ensuring that machine learning models are transparent, fair, and accountable will be essential to preventing these unintended consequences and building public trust in the technology.

In addition to addressing bias, African governments will need to develop regulatory frameworks that can keep pace with the rapid development of machine learning technologies. Policymakers will need to work closely with industry stakeholders, international organizations, and civil society to create policies that promote innovation while protecting individuals' rights and ensuring the responsible use of AI. This will include developing guidelines for data privacy, algorithmic transparency, and accountability, as well as ensuring that machine learning models are subject to appropriate oversight and evaluation. Given the cross-sectoral nature of machine learning, it will be important for regulators to collaborate across industries, ensuring that policies are consistent and aligned with broader development goals.

Another important challenge for the future of machine learning in Africa is the issue of data. Machine learning models rely on large amounts of data to function effectively, but in many parts of Africa, data is still scarce or difficult to access. Investments in data collection and data-sharing infrastructure will be critical to ensure that machine learning models are trained on high-quality, representative datasets. Governments, businesses, and research institutions will need to work together to develop open data platforms that allow for the sharing of data across sectors, while also ensuring that individuals' privacy is protected. By improving access to data, African countries can unlock the full potential of machine learning and create more robust and effective solutions to the continent's challenges.

The role of partnerships and collaboration will also be key to the future success of machine learning in Africa. Many of the most successful machine learning applications in Africa have been the result of collaboration between governments, private sector companies, non-governmental organizations, and international development agencies. These partnerships have provided the resources, expertise, and infrastructure needed to scale machine learning solutions and ensure that they are accessible to all. As machine learning continues to evolve, it will be important to foster even greater collaboration across sectors to ensure that the technology is used in ways that benefit society.

In conclusion, the future of machine learning in Africa is filled with incredible opportunities to drive economic growth, improve public services, and enhance the quality of life for millions of people. By expanding digital infrastructure, fostering AI research and development, and investing in education and regulatory frameworks, African countries can unlock the full potential of machine learning and position themselves as leaders in the global AI ecosystem. While challenges such as bias, data availability, and regulatory oversight must be addressed, the opportunities for machine learning to promote inclusive development and create a more prosperous future for Africa are vast. The next decade promises to be a period of rapid innovation and growth, with machine learning playing an increasingly important role in shaping the continent's future.

15

Unlocking Africa's Potential with Machine Learning

As we reflect on the growing role of machine learning in Africa, it becomes clear that this technology has the potential to profoundly transform the continent across various sectors. From agriculture and healthcare to finance, education, and energy, machine learning is already making significant strides, addressing some of Africa's most pressing challenges and creating new opportunities for growth and development. The future promises even more, as machine learning continues to evolve and expand, providing African countries with the tools they need to drive innovation, improve public services, and build more sustainable economies.

One of the key themes that has emerged throughout this exploration is the importance of data. Machine learning thrives on data, and ensuring that African markets have access to high-quality, reliable datasets will be essential to unlocking the full potential of this technology. Investments in digital infrastructure, data collection systems, and data-sharing platforms will be critical to providing the foundation needed for machine learning to function effectively. Without access to accurate and comprehensive data, the ability of machine learning models to generate meaningful insights and deliver tangible results will be limited. Governments, businesses, and research institutions must work together to create the necessary infrastructure that will enable data-driven innovation across the continent.

Equally important is the need to ensure that data is used responsibly and ethically. As machine learning becomes more integrated into African economies and societies, protecting individuals' privacy and ensuring the ethical use of data will be paramount. Strong data protection laws, coupled with robust enforcement mechanisms, will be needed to ensure that personal data is handled securely and that individuals retain control over how their data is used. Policymakers must establish clear guidelines that promote transparency, fairness, and accountability in the use of machine learning, ensuring that technology benefits all segments of society while safeguarding individual rights.

Another critical theme is the role of education and skill development in driving machine learning innovation. As machine learning becomes more central to Africa's economic and social landscape, there will be an increasing demand for skilled professionals who can develop, manage, and apply these technologies. Building a strong pipeline of talent will require collaboration between governments, educational institutions, and the private sector, as well as investments in training and reskilling programs that prepare workers for the jobs of the future. By cultivating a skilled workforce, African countries can ensure that they remain competitive in the global AI ecosystem and that their citizens could participate fully in the digital economy.

At the same time, it is essential that machine learning is deployed in ways that promote inclusive development. Africa's diverse economies, cultures, and communities present unique opportunities for machine learning to create solutions that address local needs and challenges. Whether it's improving agricultural productivity in rural areas, expanding access to healthcare for underserved populations, or providing financial services to individuals who are excluded from the formal banking system, machine learning has the potential to bridge the gap between urban and rural areas and ensure that all Africans benefit from the technology. However, ensuring that machine learning solutions are accessible and affordable for everyone will require concerted efforts from governments, businesses, and development organizations to create inclusive policies and programs.

The future of machine learning in Africa also brings significant challenges, particularly in the areas of bias, transparency, and regulation. Ensuring that machine learning models are fair, transparent, and accountable will be crucial to building public trust in these technologies. Machine learning systems must be rigorously tested to ensure that they do not perpetuate harmful biases or produce outcomes that disproportionately disadvantage certain groups. At the same time, regulators must develop frameworks that can keep pace with the rapid advancement of machine learning technologies, ensuring that policies are in place to protect individuals and promote the responsible use of AI. Collaboration between industry stakeholders, policymakers, and civil society will be essential to developing regulations that strike the right balance between innovation and ethics.

Looking ahead, the future of machine learning in Africa is bright. The continent has the potential to become a leader in the global AI revolution, leveraging its youthful population, diverse markets, and growing digital infrastructure to drive innovation and create new opportunities for growth. As African countries continue to embrace digital transformation, machine learning will play an increasingly important role in shaping their economic, social, and environmental futures. From improving food security and healthcare access to promoting financial inclusion and supporting sustainable development, machine learning offers solutions that can help

Africa address some of its most pressing challenges while unlocking new possibilities for progress.

In conclusion, machine learning represents a powerful tool for unlocking Africa's potential and building a more prosperous, equitable, and sustainable future. By investing in data infrastructure, fostering education and skill development, promoting inclusive policies, and ensuring that machine learning is used responsibly, African countries can harness the full power of this technology to drive positive change across the continent. The journey toward realizing the full potential of machine learning in Africa is just beginning, and the opportunities for innovation, growth, and development are boundless. The time to act is now, and by embracing machine learning, Africa can chart a course toward a brighter future for generations to come

ABOUT THE BOOK

In Machine Learning in African Markets, we embark on an insightful journey through one of the most transformative technologies of our time, machine learning and its growing impact on the African continent. As Africa embraces the digital age, machine learning offers an unprecedented opportunity to solve some of the region's most pressing challenges across industries such as agriculture, healthcare, finance, and energy. This book delves into real-world applications of machine learning in Africa, highlighting its potential to drive innovation, improve livelihoods, and foster economic growth from optimizing farming techniques to improving access to healthcare in remote areas, Machine Learning in African Markets explores the success stories of how African companies and organizations are using data-driven technologies to make a difference. The book also addresses the unique opportunities and challenges that African markets present for machine learning, including the importance of data infrastructure, education, regulatory frameworks, and inclusivity in development.

With optimism, caution, and a clear understanding of the power of machine learning, this book shines a light on the path ahead, showing how Africa can harness technology to unlock its full potential and create a brighter future for all.

www.ingramcontent.com/pod-product-compliance
Lightning Source LLC
LaVergne TN
LVHW091536070526
838199LV00001B/83